YOU'RE IN CANADA NOW . . .

MOTHERFUCKER

YOU"RE IN CANADA NOW . . .
MOTHERFUCKER

SUSAN MUSGRAVE

thistledown press

Library and Archives Canada Cataloguing in Publication

Musgrave, Susan, 1951–
You're in Canada now– : a memoir of sorts / Susan Musgrave.

ISBN 1-894345-95-9

1. Musgrave, Susan, 1951– 2. Authors, Canadian (English)–20th century–Biography. I. Title.

PS8576.U7Z477 2005   C818'.5403   C2005-904852-2

Cover and book design by Jackie Forrie
Printed in Canada

Thistledown Press Ltd.
633 Main Street, Saskatoon, Saskatchewan, S7H 0J8
www.thistledown.sk.ca

 Canada Council   Conseil des Arts
for the Arts   du Canada

 Canadian   Patrimoine
Heritage   canadien

Thistledown Press gratefully acknowledges the financial assistance of the Canada Council for the Arts, the Saskatchewan Arts Board, and the Government of Canada through the Book Publishing Industry Development Program for its publishing program.

ACKNOWLEDGMENTS

My thanks to Seán Virgo, my dedicated editor, who took time off marking papers just to work on this book. For his friendship, too, his loyalty, kindness, wit, sensitivity, perfect cups of coffee and unconditional armloads of wood.

Many of these essays were first published in the following newspapers and magazines:
Border Crossings; *Capilano Review*; *CBC Newsworld Online*; *Focus*; *In 2 Print*; *NOW Magazine*; *Ryerson Review of Journalism*; salon.com; *Saturday Night*; the *Calgary Herald*; *The Globe and Mail*; the *Ottawa Citizen*; the *Vancouver Sun*; the *Victoria Times Colonist*; *Vice*.

And in the following anthologies:
"Junkie Libido" in *Desire In Seven Voices*, edited by Lorna Crozier (D&M);

"How Do We Know Beauty When We See it" in *The Eye in the Thicket*, edited by Seán Virgo, (Thistledown Press);

"I Told You When I Came I Was a Stranger" in *Without a Guide: Women on Travel Writing*, edited by Katherine Govier, (HarperCollins);

"The Name and Nature of Poetry" in *Lost Classics* edited by Michael Ondaatje and others, (Knopf);

"Fifteen Years" in *Life As We Know it: A Collection of Personal Essays*, edited by Jennifer Foote Sweeney, (Washington Square Press);

"Remembering Al Purdy" in *Al Purdy: Essays on His Works*, edited by Linda Rogers, (Guernica Writers Series);

"When We Get There Can I Smoke?" in *bill bisset: Essays on His Works*, edited by Linda Rogers, (Guernica Writers Series).

CONTENTS

JUNKIE LIBIDO

The Particular

HEROIN CHRISTMAS

The Personal

YOU'RE IN CANADA NOW, MOTHERFUCKER

The Political

CANADIAN PSYCHO

The Professional

HOSTAGES FOR COFFEE

The Penitent

A GRIEF OBSERVED

The Posthumous

If you've read this far
this is to say thank you . . .
for everything you've taught me
including never judge a book by its title

To my mother

JUNKIE LIBIDO

The Particular

JUNKIE LIBIDO

At the age of fourteen I found my virginity. No sacred spring gushed forth to mark the spot, though years later the University of Victoria erected its Faculty of Law where my blood had stained the grass.

I had to lose it to discover what it was. After wading through nocturnal emissions in Guidance (boys had them in their dreams; girls didn't), and touching on the vulva and the vagina, "Labia minora" sounded like a Mediterranean island. I don't think the clitoris — the word or the elusive organ — was in any kind of usage back then.

Our counsellor told us, too, that girls were supposed to save themselves for "the right man". I couldn't wait. After my brown-eyed boy wormed, poked, prodded, stabbed, tore, ripped, thrust, and otherwise negotiated his way inside the place I'd dubbed "down there", he called my name. I knew he didn't expect me to answer: some things you know, and the rest you learn by finding out. Later, after apologizing for what he'd done, he kissed me and bicycled home. Alone under the budding trees I reached between my thighs to feel where our wetness had dried, tight and shiny like a scar.

The next afternoon, in an old boathouse smelling of high tide, fish and water rats, he taught me how to light a banana slug on fire, how to make it melt into a pool of sticky ooze. Then he undid his zipper and pulled out his penis, and I thought for a terrible moment he wanted me to light it on fire, to even the score for what he had done to me in the woods. Instead he said, "Put your mouth on it," and when I did it grew thicker and harder until I felt my mouth fill with a hot gush of thick, salty fluid. I thought I'd cut him with my tooth, the crooked one my parents could never afford to have straightened. His penis started shrinking right away; I thought I must have a mouthful of his blood. I had split him open and drained him and now he was shrivelling like the unlucky banana slug. I wanted to spit, but, having been brought up properly, I swallowed instead. I figured now we'd have to hitch a ride to Emergency. How was I going to explain the presence of my mouth in a boy's private region, let alone draining him and swallowing the evidence?

"I've cut you," I said. "I think I got an artery."

Then he said, his fucky brown eyes more open to me than ever, "That wasn't blood, sweetheart."

All spring and summer long we consumed each other, making love in forests and in fields, in broom closets, on chesterfields in rich peoples' houses where I babysat, in spring rain, on railway tracks, in Chinatown back alleys, on mossy rocks smelling of wild onions, up against the perimeter fence surrounding our junior high school after reading bedroom scenes torn from Henry Miller's *Sexus*. When I had my first orgasm I thought sex had driven me insane, that I was going to drown in the rogue wave of terrible pleasure that rolled over my body and pulled me down in a libidinous undertow. I didn't care. Sex was worth dying for, not just once but over and over. For a feeling this completely sweet and sad and good it would be worth spending the rest of my life locked up in a mental hospital.

But with desire came loss and fear: loss of innocence and fear that the pleasure would have to end. My best friend's mother had told her she would get cancer if she let a boy touch her breasts. It wouldn't happen immediately; it might take years for the cells to begin multiplying all out of control. I had let a boy do a lot more than get to first base, and when I missed my period, I decided I must be terminally ill.

I spent hours in my bedroom composing odes to myself, trying to come up with some pithy epitaph for my headstone, one my friends would forever remember me by, like ALWAYS. Back then ALWAYS wasn't the brand name of a female sanitary product. No odour-free pantiliner would come between my white cotton panties and the hot, earthy, ocean-ripe smell of my pent-up juices and desires.

When "the curse" came, a full day later than usual, my boy and I made love again in a graveyard. (We believed lust had made us invisible.) Part of me, I promised, would always belong to him. But even as I spoke, in my heart I felt a hot, secret tugging to be somewhere else. I was too young to be tied down. I wanted to play the field.

My parents agreed: a girl my age should be dating all kinds of different boys, especially the type who played rugby and called my father "sir", the ones from well-to-do families. These well-bred boys always respected me too much to go all the way. They respected, that is, the boundaries they had drawn to protect themselves, which meant no cheap excursions to *Labia minora* or other foreign parts requiring, in their minds, the passport of marriage, or at least a temporary entry visa.

Because I desired, I made myself desirable, wearing what I perceived to be the trappings: see-through blouses, black leather boots that reached for my thighs, a mini-skirt the size of a heating pad my mother said "left nothing to the imagi-nation". She, on the other hand, could imagine everything, especially the worst. Freedom did not mean the freedom to

SUSAN MUSGRAVE

become anything I chose, she said, meaning a nymphomaniac
(what girls who enjoyed sex were called in those days, girls
with normal healthy appetites by today's standards). The
"maniac" part I could live up to, but "nympho" made me
sound like the town pump.) To cool my desires, my parents
shipped me off to California to spend the summer sun-
worshipping with my wealthy godmother, who lived alone in
an isolated hacienda in the hills above Sacramento.

My summer rehabilitation was cut short when my
godmother caught me sunbathing beneath a blond, blue-eyed
California surfer who'd come home to the hills to pump gas
for the summer; she sent me and my sunscreen packing,
saying I had a mind of my own and was clearly oversexed. I
needed help with both these tragedies, everyone seemed to
think. My parents had me committed to a mental hospital.

The kindred spirits I met there called the institution the
"Garden of Eden", because even in this healing environment
of group and shock therapy, sex was everybody's downfall.
The apple of my eye was a three-hundred-pound, thirty-eight-
year-old absent-minded professor from California. When my
parents threatened to have him charged with statutory rape,
we fled to Berkeley — leaving behind his wife and four kids
— escaping from the mental hospital by exiting through a
door marked ENTRANCE ONLY. "Who will ever marry her
now?" my Victorian father said.

He needn't have worried: my desire was never for marriage.
Desire was two bodies banging together in the dark, leaping
from a burning plane without a parachute, diving into the
wreckage of ourselves and finding parts of our bodies no one
had ever discovered or named, reinventing the future. I desired
only, and always, to be desired.

I stayed with my professor until I felt it again — that hot, secret tugging — to be somewhere else. Back home, in the country where I belonged, I found someone new. And after this new someone came another, and another. As I grew older, I became less and less discriminating. I was an attraction addict, and when you need a quick fix, you stop being choosy. I no longer believed there was any part of me left to save for any man, even the wrong one. Falling in love became the gauze I applied over the wet wound of the heart, and love, my heart-stopper drug. When romance started to look iffy, and passion turned to depression and despair, I would begin my search all over again. Any man was the right man as long as he could jump-start my junkie libido.

There is, of course, a scientific explanation for this emotional disturbance we call desire. Some experts maintain that we "fall in love" when the neurons in our limbic system, our emotional core, become saturated by a small molecule called phenylethylamine, or PEA, and other naturally occurring amphetamines. High on this organic brain "speed", lovers stay awake all night talking about the future, reliving the past, falling in giddy love with each other, and with themselves, over and over again. The slightest thought of your sweetheart — a letter in the mail, a phone message, the mention of his name — sends a tsunami of exhilaration through the brain. You quit eating, lose weight, get pimples. (I *know* it's true love when my face breaks out.) The hermit you always thought you were wakes up each day delirious, gregarious, in an optimistic, euphoric, stuttering, agonizing, blissful, *adjectivey* state. Love, we say, is to die for. As if there can be nothing better, nothing hotter or holier on earth.

It would be too simple to say that desire — this neural itch, this alert, intoxicating, deep, mystical devotion to another human being — is due solely to natural stimulants in the brain. But understanding what made me so strung-out then leaves me feeling less like a prisoner of my desire than a hostage with enough information to negotiate my way through a neurochemical jungle. For if desire is what happens when you're flying on natural speed, brain chemistry can be held responsible for the end of the affair, also. Either the brain endings adapt and are no longer affected by the onslaught of amphetamines, or the levels of PEA begin to drop. The brain can't go on forever in this heightened state of etherized romantic bliss. Your brain wants to get you off one kind of drug — and onto another.

As the excitement and novelty subside (anywhere between eighteen months and three years after attraction begins), a natural morphine-like substance kicks in that calms the mind. As these endorphins surge through the brain they usher in the second phase of love: attachment, bringing with it the sensations of security and peace. But if you're like I used to be — craving the constant high induced by insecurity and war, and not yet ready for morphine-surrender, the cool dependable fires of attachment — you'll do what I did over and over again: break the bonds of love and abandon the idea of becoming permanently attached to anyone.

Psychopharmacologists argue that the motivation to achieve an altered mood or consciousness is a "fourth drive", as much a part of the human condition, and as important to most other species as sex, thirst and hunger. During the Vietnam War water buffalo were observed nibbling on opium poppies more often than they do in times of peace, the same way the American soldiers, fighting the Viet Cong, took to using heroin.

From caffeine and Graham Wafers to marijuana and heroin, most of us use drugs for one purpose: to change our mood, to medicate ourselves when we feel overburdened by twenty-first century life.

I remember a dinner party back in the mid-seventies, where our host passed around a human skull before dessert, collecting donations for an eightball of cocaine, a bottle of Irish Whiskey — whatever we could score out there in the world of the living. Later, when we had all scooped a couple of grams of glitter into the drains of our waiting nostrils, I sat on the beach in front of the house with my friend Tom York, who abstained, while he talked about his desire for "desirelessness". Tom, who'd moved from Arkansas to the BC wilderness during the Vietnam War, was a United Church minister who read Heidegger before breakfast, a writer who killed and ate a bear for his fortieth birthday, a weightlifter who could deadlift three hundred pounds, a marathon runner, a philanderer — when anyone accused him of being immoral in his pursuits of the flesh, he reminded them not to confuse religion with morality — and a gentleman. The last time I saw him before he was killed on an interstate highway, he played Percy Sledge singing "When a Man Loves a Woman" for me in Waterloo, Ontario. Tom used to say I was unique among the women he knew, because I had never desired him in the ways a woman most often desires a man. Flattery was Tom's Southern way of engaging in social intercourse.

Back then I argued: to be desireless was to be dead. Tom just listened and nodded his head and drew on the pipe he smoked. I said I couldn't remember a time when desire wasn't wailing in my veins, wetting the insides of my thighs all the way up into the Bermuda Triangle between my legs where the man I loved always disappeared, eventually. Then I would begin my quest again, running up long-distance phone bills and changing continents as often as I changed my underwear, my phone number, my address, my eating habits, my sleeping patterns. Desire kept me in the wind and on fire, burning wild, out of control, and in need of a search party to find my own self after a night in bed with some — in retrospect — wholly insignificant other.

Tom's novel, *Desireless*, was published posthumously. I know now that Tom wasn't talking only about sexual desire, though his wife had named thirty-nine co-respondents when she'd petitioned for a divorce. I wish he were still alive so we could laugh about my naïveté. How long and hard I argued about something Tom (not to mention the Buddhists, and Freud) had always understood. That desire is the cause of all suffering: that we are never so defenceless against suffering as when we love.

I had promised my first love a part of me would always be his. A part of me has kept the promise I made. Some nights I dream of my brown-eyed boy, our last time together in the long grass in that graveyard where we thought lust had made us invisible. When he opens his eyes I am gone, and on the headstone that was our pillow, my epitaph: "Behold, Desire!"

I TOLD YOU WHEN I CAME I WAS A STRANGER

My first marriage began to crumble around the time I developed the habit of dipping Graham Wafers in my morning cup of tea. (Perhaps it was a coincidence, but as Jung said, if traced back far enough, coincidence becomes inevitable.) After being dunked in the cup that cheers but does not inebriate, the crackers get mushy and can be swallowed without being masticated. We drink liquids and we chew solids, but I've never found a word for the way tea-infused Graham Wafers are ingested.

In the early days of my first marriage I permitted myself only four Graham Wafers each morning, with my first cup of tea; later, when my husband began to obsess about my compulsive behaviour, I stopped counting. By then I'd noticed, too, a change in my libido.

With a little research it was easy to find out where my favourite tea, the Iron Goddess of Mercy, is grown: on the slopes of Amoy, China, where it is hand-picked by specially trained monkeys. Graham Wafers were invented in the early 1800s by Sylvester Graham, who served them to children in his boardinghouse because he believed it stopped them from abusing themselves. But does anyone really know where the libido comes from? The *Gage Canadian* says its origin is the Latin *libido*, meaning desire, but that's the *word*, not the thing: the thing that appears out of nowhere, rising and floating, lighter than air.

When I learned about Sylvester Graham's motives in dishing out wafers to his wards — as a child I, too, had pleasured myself by immersing Graham Wafers in my Bunnikins mug full of milk — I began to suspect the soggy biscuits might have something to do with the decline and fall of my own sexual urges. But even this knowledge didn't stop me. I craved more and more. Some mornings I ate so many Graham Wafers I wasn't able to force down the breakfast my good-hearted husband had laid out for me.

My husband was a criminal lawyer defending five Americans and eighteen Colombians charged with smuggling thirty tonnes of marijuana into Canada. When they'd run out of rolling papers, they'd brought their ship in for supplies on the west coast of Vancouver Island. The same day I ate an entire box of Graham Wafers, dropping each straight into the pot without taking the trouble to pour myself a cup of tea first, the jury acquitted the smugglers, and one of them, the future father of my child, walked out of the courthouse wearing an unbleached linen suit and a T-shirt that said "I SCORED".

I offered him a ride. To South America, or as far as we could go. I was ready to give up my Graham Wafer habit and start afresh, I said. On the steps of the courthouse I looked at him and saw, in the gleam of his own shadowy eyes, a depth of wanting that promised heaven. It wasn't until years later I realized that the desire must have been my own reflected back, that the promise I thought I saw had been nothing more than the neglected spirit of my own lust.

We knew little about each other, but mystery, unknowing, is energy. We crossed the border with Leonard Cohen singing *It's true that all the men you knew were dealers who said they were through with dealing every time you gave them shelter* on KISS-FM. In Sudden Valley we camped by a fire in the night and drank white rum from a bottle inside a bag. Paul showed me his tattoo — a pair of faded lips, as if a ghost wearing lipstick had kissed him above his left nipple. I kissed his lips. In the morning we flew the Whisperliner Jet Service to Atlanta. I'd signed on for the duration.

In Miami Beach we danced in a cabaret where two blonde sisters sang other people's songs. We made love, that first night, in a vegetarian hotel. When we checked out, the desk clerk told me even if you take a bath every day you can't wash your heart.

I remember the day so clearly because it was the first turning point in our life together. At the Bounty Hotel in Coconut Grove I overheard Paul on the bathroom telephone talking to his former girlfriend in Texas; he said she was giving him a big erection. As my mother would have said, "the honeymoon was over". I thought of turning back as I walked the streets alone, back to the predictable life I'd left, my husband asleep in his overstuffed chair, empty wine glass in hand, and "Emotional Rescue" turning soundlessly on the stereo. When I'd called to say I had left with Paul he accused me of being a "ruiner", said all I'd ever fulfilled were his worst fears. But I'd wanted the strange and the wild and wasn't ready to turn my back on a world I hadn't explored yet. I wrote postcards to friends, quoting the poet Caesar Vallejo. "What can I do but change my style of weeping?"

My friends, I knew, could not understand why I had abandoned a loyal husband to follow some dealer into some troubled Latin American regime. I finally came up with an answer while watching the film *Tootsie* on the plane from Miami to Panama. Jessica Lange was explaining a similar predicament: "There are a lot of men out there. I am very selective. I look around to see who can give me the worst time, and I choose him."

In Panama we changed hotels every other day, registering each time under a different name, in case we were being followed. When we ran out of hotels, Paul found a penthouse with a view of the Panama Canal, overlooking a walled garden filled with orange-blossoming trees, vines that dripped a lavender scented moss, and bougainvillea. It was paradise, but beyond our means. In the heart of the banking district Paul rented a basement apartment, instead, with a view of the House of Carnage where I could buy meat. Our landlord called his building "The Elite" for reasons that were not apparent. Marisol, his wife, gave us a termite-infested sofa that gave way into a bed, and a desk lamp that gave me electrical shocks. But at least we had a mailing address. My mother wrote saying she was "puzzled by our freedom of choice for place of domicile, which is usually determined by the husband's place of work."

Paul's work took him south for *negocios delicados;* he came back with the souvenirs he'd bought for me in airport giftshops: a silver llama brooch, a Peruvian devil-dancer, a Panama hat. To make it up to me for having stayed away so long, he'd whisk me into the hills to eat at a restaurant called The Godfather where the river had washed away part of the dining room, then up the coast to Punta Charme where we'd walk the night beach, black water dragging the shingle back.

Each time he went away he was gone for longer. I explored Panama City on my own, rising early to buy arepas on the streets as the bootblacks were opening their stalls under the colonnades. I'd wash the buns down with thick sweet coffee sitting in a booth at Manolo's reading about Colombia in the *Miami Herald*, stories of the sicarios from the barrios who kill for the cocaine cartels for as little as $100 a hit. I took Spanish lessons at the YMCA in the Canal Zone. One taxi driver, his face like polished black hardwood, took me the long way, through the slums. He unzipped his trousers, using sign language to demonstrate his desire to join me for sexual inter-course in the back seat. I told him the only line I'd learned at my lesson. *"Mi esposa toca el piano muy bien —* My wife plays the piano very well." He got the impression I was a *loca*, and drove me straight to the Zone without further deviation.

Esas ollas, que bonitos, como brilliant. At the Y I also learned the words housewives needed in order to communicate with their maids. "These pots, how pretty, how they shine." There were times I wished I were part of their world, with a fixed address and children who took piano lessons after school, and a man who read the stock market quotations over breakfast instead of one who flew standby from Bogota with powder burns on his body and a stomach full of condoms packed with cocaine.

Desperate for someone to talk to, I befriended a Panamanian I'd seen every morning sitting in the booth across from mine at Manolo's. He also read the *Miami Herald*, English edition. John Jesus worked in pharmaceuticals, and owned a different coloured Mercedes for every day of the week. He drove me to the beach at Vera Cruz where we sat in partially submerged deck-chairs under a sign saying WARNING SHARK INFESTED WATERS drinking exotic cocktails that came in a baby's bottle with a nipple. There he confided in me about his difficult but beautiful American girlfriend. He had attended a seminar in body language and could tell true emotion when someone was weeping because the veins would stand up on her hands. When Jesus bought his girlfriend a silver BMW for her birthday, she'd cried, but her veins had stayed submerged. He wondered if he should have given her a gold Mercedes instead.

I couldn't advise him. I told him, instead, about my own unsettled love life: whenever I asked Paul why I couldn't join him in Colombia, he told me it was too dangerous. As a *gringa* I would be an obvious target for kidnappers.

Jesus said Paul should hire a bodyguard, my own personal Uzi man. But Colombia remained too dangerous for me right up until the day I discovered a sharp red fingernail clipping in Paul's trouser pocket. Then he confessed. The danger was Elizabeth.

He described her, over the phone, how her hands felt hot to the touch (he complained that mine were always cold), how she was "something of a poet herself" and had won a prize at high school. That night I packed and booked a flight to Vancouver. But Paul arrived before my plane left and told me, over "Mired Seafood" at The Godfather, that he was trying hard not to fall in love with Elizabeth. I heard, in the back of my pounding head, Leonard Cohen singing *I told you when I came I was a stranger*. I wanted to say fair enough, we had never promised each other everlasting love, but my heart had shrivelled into a fist and I struck him instead.

"I wish you could meet the person who causes you so much unhappiness," Paul said, when we'd both recovered.

It's been said that those who do not see themselves as victims accept the greater stress. I had never thought of myself as a victim; I told Paul I wanted to meet Elizabeth, and that I was willing to accept responsibility for the consequences. The next morning he gave notice on our apartment. He paid Marisol $600 towards the phone bill, which left $500 owing. Marisol kissed me goodbye. I think she had grown fond of me, or perhaps felt sorry for me mixed up in a life where I was being "dragged about" from continent to continent — as she must have perceived it — by a man who didn't pay his phone bills on time.

Paul flew back to Colombia ahead of me. I said goodbye to Jesus who was convinced I was going to Colombia to execute Elizabeth. Colombian prisons were very inhospitable, he said, and gave me the card of a lawyer in Bogota who would be able to fix things with the judge.

∼ ∼ ∼

I asked the Avianca agent for an aisle seat over the wing in the non-smoking section of the aircraft. I got the middle seat in the back row between a chain smoker and the Panamanian I'd pinched going through immigration because he'd butted in.

I peered past the Panamanian in the window seat, saying goodbye to the freighters lined up at sea waiting to enter the Canal, and to the vultures over the Hilton. On the far side of the steamy runway there were bananas strung out along a clothesline, which reminded me that I had forgotten to call home to ask my husband to pick up the drycleaning I'd left behind in Sidney two months ago. Beneath the wing a group of baggage handlers hunched together with two men dressed as pilots, sharing a cigarette.

"You see that?" said the Panamanian. "They are smoking drugs. It is probably why we are late." He introduced himself, and gave me his card. Julio was in the "international market". "So the pilot gets drugs and steers us into the Andes, no problem." he said. "Everyone in Colombia is a pilot." He went on to recommend that I always buy my drugs from the police. "They get them for nothing, so they can sell them cheap."

In Bogota I had a three-hour stopover and I fell asleep in the Telecom room, the one dimly-lit area of the airport. When

I opened my eyes a policeman was standing over me, holding an oily lunchbag. He wore his white gun-belt aslant, cowboy-style.

"*Esta enferma?*" he asked. He reached into his bag and pulled out a fistful of greasy pork-scratchings.

I told him I wasn't sick, just sleepy. He munched on his *chicarrones* for awhile and then asked to see my papers.

"You are very far from home. Your husband is not with you?" he asked in rapid Spanish, his fat eyes circling my breasts. He stuffed his bag of pork-rinds in his trouser pocket as two more officers, one a woman dressed in a bottle green suit, her skirt slit up the side, headed my way. The officer asked his boss permission to look through my purse; the *jefe* shrugged and I handed it over to the policewoman. "*Hay una problema?*" I asked her. She patted her revolver. It wasn't the answer I'd been hoping for.

The *jefe* thumbed through my passport. When he smiled he showed two teeth rimmed with gold. "You are a Canadian citizen?" he asked. He spoke English without the trace of an accent.

I felt cold, all of a sudden, and for the first time noticed the bad smell in the terminal, half-diesel, half-human. By the door a *campesina* was selling oranges she had built up into a little pyramid. The *jefe* walked over and helped himself to one, broke it in half and offered me a section.

"In Canada," he said, applying his mouth to his orange half and sucking the juices out, "I have a brother who is in prison." Then, spitting a seed, he dropped the sucked-dry orange peel on the floor.

The other two officers had taken apart my fountain pen, searching for contraband. Neither of them looked happy about the black ink on their hands. At the bottom of my purse, in a pink plastic case, they found a tampon — one designed by a woman gynaecologist that didn't come with an applicator. They eyed me, triumphantly.

Then they began to speak fast, rolling the tampon over in their hands. I looked at the *jefe*, and tried shrugging. I had "travel insurance", in the form a hundred dollar American bill in my wallet, but I didn't know if a bribe was necessary yet. The officer with the pork-rinds held the tampon in his palm, and began unwrapping it. The *jefe* kept his eyes on me while the woman kept an ink-stained hand on her gun.

The officer had the tampon dangling by its blue string. I gave the *jefe* a look so much as to say he was a man of the world, he understood this business, then I took a risk. I nodded towards the officer who was swinging the tampon around in a slow circle. "Next he'll be wanting to use it," I said.

The *jefe* had another moment of blankness before his face doubled up into a grin. The others caught on, and began snickering, too, as if they thought some joke had been made at the *gringa*'s expense. The *jefe* continued to grin, handed me back my Tourist Card and my passport, and pointed me in the direction of the departure lounge.

"She is not a tourist," I heard him say, as I left.

∽ ∽ ∽

The Hotel Desaguadero was not the luxury hotel I'd been hoping for, but it was the only one in town with vacancies, Paul had explained, as we drove in from the airport.

"*Desaguadero*" meant "drain": the road down to the hotel was impassable by car. The owner looked surprised to see us and asked Paul how we had chanced upon the place, as if it were impossible that anyone might come to his hotel by choice. In the evening he served chicken necks, rice with gravel, and Coca-Cola on a patio under a crackling bug-zapper; the scorched remains of flying insects fluttered down onto our plates. When a royalty cheque arrived from Canada we were able to afford a month's rent on an apartment with a view of the Andes' western chain.

Elizabeth was not the femme fatale I'd been expecting, either. I'd been prepared to hate her; I'd pictured her taller than me, full of sophisticated talk about punting in Brazil, cigarette smouldering from an ivory holder. But even in red stilettos she didn't reach my armpits. She wore a Snoopy watch and chewed gum non-stop. "I dream of air conditioning and international cuisine," she repeated, practising "the King's English" on me.

Elizabeth went out of her way to try and please me. She carried my shopping bags when the three of us went to the market where I bought jet black maize, basil, wild strawberries and a bouquet of cream-coloured freesias. On a sidewalk two *bruhas* had laid out luck charms and magical prescriptions. Paul found a protein powder that was meant for expectant mothers. Elizabeth made a joke about her fat stomach, and said maybe she had a baby inside. I said, rather sternly, "Whose?" "*Anonimo*," she replied, as I lingered by the monkey fetuses used as ritual abortifacients.

When we'd settled in our apartment I invited Elizabeth for dinner. She asked to read some of my poetry and, to be polite, I asked her what she did for a living. Elizabeth worked for MAS — *Muerte a Secuestradores*, literally "Death to Kidnappers", the Colombian equivalent to the Rotary Club, she tried to assure me. She was committed to doing only good deeds for the community, like the time she smuggled a grenade in her vagina into Bella Vista prison and blew up forty notorious *secuestradores*. She spoke as casually about killing people as she did about my culinary skills: when I made a pesto sauce she said basil was used in sorcery, never in cooking. I made the further mistake of adding the wrong kind of cheese to my pesto so that the mixture turned into a slimy green ball. Paul tossed the bewitched sauce in the river as we walked to the Avenida Sexta to see a film about French chefs eating themselves to death. Afterwards we stopped at a *Churrascaria* for *rachitas*. The shoeshine boys asked for our leftovers, then hunkered down on their shoe boxes in a little circle, feasting on our picked-over ribs.

Elizabeth insisted on repaying us with "Colombian hospitality", and, on a feast day in honour of Our Virgin of Mercy, invited us to her house in the Barrio Popular. In the living room she seated us under a bleeding heart of Jesus and a poster of Pablo Escobar with the slogan "I'll never run away." We drank beer she had brewed from maracuya, yeast, bananas, and blackberries. I was on my third glass when Elizabeth began laughing at me and speaking to Paul in Spanish. "Of course it gives you damn diarrhoea, but who says an evening of happiness isn't worth a bit of shit?" Paul translated. After the beer Elizabeth served *mondongo*, a stew made from rice with tripe, which Paul raved about. "We must have this recipe," he said. The smell made me sick. I went to the door for fresh air and stood under a horseshoe and an aloe vera sprig (both for good luck). After watching a gang of children firing at each other with imaginary machine guns, I broke off a piece of the aloe plant for Paul; he'd had nothing but bad luck in his business lately. When I went to sit down again I heard him talking to Elizabeth about moving his operation further south again to Bolivia.

When the time came I helped him pack his suitcase, which always smelled of coffee. And then, I don't know why, I started

to weep. Paul asked me if I thought something was ending —
he was worried, also; he said he saw himself huddled in a
corner with the four winds hitting at him, and didn't know
how to get out. I drove him to the airport in his linen suit and
the T-shirt he always wore when he travelled, but the words I
SCORED had faded in the wash and were almost unreadable.

I woke up the next day still feeling ill, and called Elizabeth
who arrived with leftover *mondongo* — a stomach settler, she
tried to convince me. I vomited for twenty-four hours; when
I stopped throwing up she drove me on the back of her motor
scooter to a clinic where a doctor diagnosed appendicitis and
said he must operate at once. I rolled off the dirty blood-
stained sheet and got dressed to go home. Judging by the
streets lined with funeral parlours surrounding the hospitals
in Cali, a hospital was a place you went to die.

The doctor gave me an injection to "help the vomiting"
and Elizabeth stayed with me over the next few days. I tried
to tell her I'd forgiven her for her love affair with Paul, but she
pretended not to understand and rattled on about how
nervous she often got, waiting to gun a kidnapper down. She'd
found a trick that seemed to help: she got a bullet, took out
the lead, and poured the gunpowder into a hot black coffee.
She drank the lot and it steadied her nerves, she said. The
subject of love, though, seemed beyond the realm of "The
King's English".

When I felt better, Elizabeth took me to see her doctor for
blood tests. The results were positive: I no longer had to risk
carrying tampons around with me in Colombia. Elizabeth
wept with happiness and made me promise she could be the
godmother.

I didn't know where to reach Paul, though Elizabeth had
kept me up-to-date on his travels (one of her brothers was in

the same business). One week he was in Santa Cruz, Bolivia, waiting for a load to come in a truck full of potatoes; the next week he was in the *llanos* making payoffs to the army. I didn't ever know what to expect from him. Only one thing was certain: I saw the funeral parlours, their window displays of tiny white coffins with twisted brass handles and crimson satin linings, and I knew I would not have my baby in Colombia. I packed my typewriter, my books, and my few clothes, then wrote a letter to Paul saying I didn't know when I'd be back. In fiction, I said, there had to be resolution; not so in life.

I booked a one-way ticket to Vancouver — in my own name. I had become so used to using aliases my own name seemed unnatural; it no longer fit. Elizabeth offered to drive me to the airport but I had too much luggage for the back of her scooter. I ordered a cab, kissed her, and threatened to send her my recipe for pesto sauce. Elizabeth hugged me, hard, and wept again when I asked her to look after Paul, whenever he made it home.

Her emotions were true — I checked. The veins were standing up on her hot, manicured hands.

WILD TIME

Every August 1st, give or take twenty-four hours, the geese return to the bay in front of my house. I know, because for the last fifteen years I've marked this, the beginning of the end of summer, on my calendar. My calendar confirms what the honking of the geese tells me — but how do the *geese* know? Is it a new shade of grey in the morning light out on the water, an August 1st-heralding sound another shorebird makes, the way the harbour seals wriggle their noses into the salt-smelling breeze? I'm beginning to wonder what I've been missing, what pleasures I've been in too much of a hurry to appreciate or even notice, by strapping some controlling measure of time onto my wrist and hanging a reminder of the coming month on my wall, X-ing off the days.

Since the industrial age time has become a measure of our productivity, and also our most valuable commodity. The onslaught of new technology that promised to set us free has instead made us slaves to our cellphones and laptop computers, which instill expectations of instantaneous action. Overall these machines fuel the trend that every nanosecond must be accounted for. We are quick to condemn those whom we perceive as "wasting their time" and surround ourselves by time-and-labour-saving devices such as my newly acquired food processor that decimates a cabbage in less time than it takes George Bush to say, "Time is running out on (sic) Osama bin Laden" (and takes the rest of the day to disassemble and clean). If I wish to walk across the road and watch the geese float out to sea, I will likely chastize myself for "getting nothing done" and for squandering my precious time. Yet, what could be more precious than living fully in those magic and spontaneous moments that make us happy to be alive?

Last summer, a friend from Ottawa accused me of having entered her into a time-warp on Vancouver Island — I asked her to take off her shoes, and her watch, when she came into my house — but why is living in harmony with the moon and tides more warped than waking to an alarm and your first thoughts being, "How much time do I have to get up, get dressed, get out the door, drop the kids at day care and get down to the House of Commons?" In the daily grind, circa 2004, we're up 365 going 24 – 7 in a heavily-weighted competition against the clock. Stopping to chat to a neighbour over the fence or slowing down to watch the geese float out to sea will only make you late for your appointment with your time management consultant.

Island time is what Jay Griffiths, author of *A Sideways Look at Time*, calls wild time. "Just as vast wilderness once surrounded us, so too, time was wild: everlasting, undefined, unenclosed, unnamed, a mystery." Time, she says, has been seized and colonized in the West; clock time — or tamed time — is a mere construct, arbitrary and artificial, of modern society. Wild time, by contrast, is an open-handed hour, the open-hearted day.

Wild time thrives in nature, and in the spirit of play (western society fears play, which includes sex, drug-taking, rock 'n' roll and other intoxicating behaviours such as art, which is serious play of a subversive nature) and every child is born exuberantly full of it. "Adults were enemies," Anne Wilkinson wrote in her memoir of her childhood summers on Lake Simcoe in Ontario, "not bitter enemies (except on occasions) but natural, inevitable ones. Their greatest offence was in regard to Time, an abstraction they did not in the least understand. They were always ringing bells or calling Time for breakfast, Time to get out of the water, Time for bed — whereas we, with a more philosophical concept of the clock, knew that Time, in their sense, did not exist. What we happened to be doing was forever, whether it was floating in the mild blue lake, or lying in bed, half asleep on a summer morning. Slowly the enemy won, and thereby robbed us of immortality. Before we knew it our own hands were shaking bells and calling Time for dinner, Time to go to bed."

Too soon we are forced to grow up, to live at the mercy of two authoritative taskmasters: the clock and the calendar. In our busy lives nothing happens if we don't plan it, often months in advance. We work full-time or part-time and wonder where the time went. We're not here for a long time, but for a good time, the saying goes — a trendier way of describing how we kill time until time kills us.

But stop for a second: look back on a near-death experience or an ecstatic night of love-making. Recall, in terrible or blissful vivid detail, how time stood still. Perhaps we all need to take time to appreciate those moments, those brief glimpses of immortality between birth and death that have nothing to do with the hands on a clock.

THE LOCAL PAPER IS CALLED *THE WORLD*

Up until recently crime in any small Vancouver Island town meant the occasional theft of a dinghy, and a criminal was someone who watered his lawn on the wrong alternate day. Times change, and a month ago we had a case of a peeping tom — he got caught beneath a couple's window, waiting — and waiting — and waiting for something to happen. He fell asleep — waiting. His snores woke *them* up, and they called the police.

My daughter wants to live in Toronto. She tells me she does not intend to spend the best years of her life "in the middle of nowhere". I was thinking of telling her that is where most of us spend most of our lives, but there's no point getting existential with someone who dyes her hair blue with Kool-Aid.

In a small town — and by small I mean one with a population of 1,100 or less — you can't get away with much because everybody knows your face, even if you're wearing a disguise.

In my town, for instance, you wouldn't dare go into a bank with a pair of pantyhose over your face because you'd be sure to be recognized . . .

"I know you . . . you bought those pantyhose on sale at Shopper's last week, you were in the line-up ahead of me and I was buying three pairs of the same only you recommended the control top and the reinforced toe . . . " the teller would say before the police arrived, and the next thing I'd know I'd be front page news in the local paper, which is called *The World*.

A few weeks ago, trying to save myself a trip to town, I called my bank to get a balance on my VISA account. I identified myself, then the woman on the other end of the line asked me a skill-testing question. She said, "How do I know you're who you say you are?"

Good question. When I couldn't come up with an answer she gave me another chance. "Tell me something about your life that I would know."

This is "Personal Touch" banking carried to an extreme. (I wonder if you'd get the same personalized service in a city?) "For instance," she continued, "tell me how your eldest daughter crawled when she was a baby."

My daughter didn't crawl on all fours, she scooted on her bum. I got the skill testing question right this time, so I held while she called up my account number on her computer. Then she said, "You don't really want to know your balance."

It wasn't a question. It was a statement. This is one of the disadvantages of living in a small town. When it comes to your own life, everyone else seems to know what's best for you.

For example, I am in the Health Food store, writing a cheque for $153 worth of organic bee-pollen based cosmetics, when the proprietor says, "Ever read *2000 years of Exploitation*? It's all about how women are exploited by the cosmetics industry."

In the butcher shop when I ask for a leg of lamb the butcher wants to know how I am going to cook it. "I was going to try something different," I venture. "Stew the meat in red wine with a bit of bay leaf and a dash of cinnamon . . . " but he's already vetoing that idea. "Just stick it in the oven," he says, shaking his head emphatically. "A little salt, maybe some garlic powder. Nothing fancy. Good meat doesn't need doctoring."

Which reminds me, I'm late for my doctor's appointment. I head back up the street and when I arrive, out of breath, at Dr. Marsh's office, his receptionist hands me a piece of paper with the word DEATH scrawled across the top, followed by three exclamation points. I am stunned. Why couldn't he at least have waited to tell me in person?

The receptionist tells me Dr. Marsh is on the phone but will be with me in a few minutes. I assume he's making arrangements with the local coroner, but no, when I press my ear to the wall I hear him making a date with his wife to go and see "Pulp Fiction" after they grab a quick bite when he's through with me.

My minutes sound definitely numbered. Then, in he saunters, carrying my chart, which is about as thick as *The History of the Decline and Fall of the Roman Empire*. "What am I seeing you about today?" he asks somewhat indifferently. When you deal with mortality on a daily basis I guess you become immune.

"You tell me, doctor. I was just hoping for those test results . . . "

"Oh, that," he says. "Didn't I phone you last week? Your blood is fine. You can stop taking the iron."

He points to the memo. "Did you like my joke?"

I look down at what I thought was his prognosis in my hand. Of course I haven't read further than the first line. I read on. "I'm not afraid of death . . . When I die I want to go in my sleep . . . just like my Grandfather did . . . not screaming like his passengers."

"That's very funny," I say.

"It's sick," he says. "I knew you'd be the only one of my patients who would possibly appreciate something that sick."

I leave his office with a new lease on life, and drive to the grocery store, waving at everyone I know. At Thrifty's I grab a couple of breadsticks for my kids, being very careful only to touch the ones I am going to buy. (It can be done.) But this curmudgeon standing next to me says, "Use the tongs. Use the tongs."

I think, what's to stop a germ from vaulting off the end of one of my fingers, scooting along the tongs and diving off onto one of the breadsticks I am not intending to buy?

I don't say that, I try to stay reasonable. "I am only touching the ones I am going to buy," I say. To which he replies, "That's what they all say."

I have this vision of a vigilante with nothing better to do than hang out in front of baked goods waiting for someone to come along who doesn't use tongs. This is a sign that my town is getting to be something bigger than small. In a really small town you'd know everyone in the grocery store and their personal hygiene habits. You'd know whether they were the sort who would have washed their hands before going grocery shopping or not.

When I get to the check-out the clerk doesn't ask me if I want paper or plastic: she knows I use plastic because I read somewhere that paper bags destroy the rain forest. Today, when I ask for paper (I need it to mail some parcels overseas) she looks at me, aghast.

The problem is that when you have a familiar face, people expect you to behave predictably. It shakes people if you do anything out of character.

"Plastic's fine," I say. Relief floods back into her face.

I am determined not to upset the status quo at the fish market. "I'll take three pounds of sockeye, filleted," I say. "As usual."

"Salmon? Again? Don't your kids get sick of it? Halibut would be a change," says the fishmonger, looking at me as if I have no imagination.

I pay for the halibut and get back in my car feeling my own life doesn't belong to me. Now I'm running on empty, also. I swing by the gas station and say, "Fill it, please . . . " but before I can say "with regular" the attendant is filling her up. With regular. I ask him if he'll please check under the hood for me because the engine has been making that funny noise again.

Everyone in this town is an expert. He disappears under the hood, then looks up at me as if I'm the one with the sick alternator.

"Ever thought of trading her in?" he asks.

AN EXCLUDED SORT OF PLACE

Crumpling an old newspaper to light a fire in the wood stove, an item catches my eye. Every day a teacher, Yang Zhengxue, treks an hour and a half up and down craggy peaks in a remote corner of southern China to reach his students who live high on a mountain ridge in a limestone cave, "an almost prehistoric habitat without electricity, running water or any other amenity that would identify it as a home for residents of the twenty-first century."

Sounds like home sweet home to me. The newspaper is dated December 11, 1983, but the news hasn't changed much. Weapons of mass misery, genocide, political blunderings — the so called real world seems a long way from these misty, mystical isles. Here, in the wilderness, I encounter a different sense of time, where my days fail to follow orderly paths, unfolding instead in unpredictable ways. I reset my body and mind to a cosmic time frame. I plan my activities around the incoming and outgoing tides, the rising and setting sun.

There is no such concept as manana on Haida Gwaii; no word exists for that kind of urgency. A tourist once stopped for Buddy — a local character who spent his days walking the five miles, back and forth, between Skidegate and Queen Charlotte City — and asked him if he needed a ride. "No thanks," Buddy replied. "I'm in a hurry."

There's no cellphone service here, no schedules to keep. Pockets of these Islands missed the last ice age, but a few of my technological, pioneering friends have recently joined the twenty-first century and bought transistor radios so they can find out the current time by tuning in to the CBC.

A few summers ago when we visited Jim Fulton (who had been NDP MP for the Skeena district for fifteen years) at his log house on the Tlell River, miles away from any "conveniences", we sat around the wood cook stove eating deer meat by gaslight. "Have you ever heard of electricity?" my citified daughter, then aged six, asked the Fultons' kids. "Well, you should *get* it!"

∽∼∽

Truth moves to the heart as slowly as a glacier, and that's how time moves here, also. I've been waiting at the side of the road with a garbage bag full of dirty laundry for most of the morning (my truck has a dead battery); the first fisherman to come by in his half-ton, stops. I settle into a pile of gill nets on the seat beside him, then ask if he has the time.

"I used to wear a watch," he says, "but I lost it in the winch." He shows me an empty sleeve. "I know one thing for sure. There'll be a high tide tonight."

The fisherman — Crabby Mike — who once rode with Sonny Barger and the Hell's Angels — came here twenty years ago. He sailed his boat up and anchored it in Masset Inlet, where it started to sink.

Mike rescued his fishing rod from below decks, and sat on the tipping deck, drinking a Bud Light, fishing. "I'd come to the Charlottes to fish," he told everyone, afterwards. "And that's just what I intended to do. Fish."

People from all walks of life come here for the fish. Our former Prime Minister visited a couple of summers ago, too, but I doubt whether Monsieur Chretien had time to visit the

Best Little Lure House in the Charlottes, in Queen Charlotte
City. He certainly didn't venture in to Haida Bucks in Masset
for a latte — he ate lunch aboard his airplane on the Masset
landing strip.

～～～

A school bus full of llamas, their heads poking out the open
windows, draws up in front of the laundromat, where Crabby
Mike deposits me. Nobody gives the llamas a second look —
they're used to it, just as people are used to living with wild
and unpredictable weather.

"But doesn't it rain *all* the time up there?" a friend,
planning a visit from Vancouver, writes. (Okay, so we're not
completely cut off: there *is* a daily mail service — providing
the plane from Vancouver can land, on a runway stretching
between two driftwood littered beaches at the Sandspit
airport.) And, yes, the rain it raineth. The rain falls so hard
here it bounces off the ground then goes back up.

It's no surprise that the windshield wipers on my pick-up
have a life of their own. Even if the rain lets up, and I reach to
switch them off, they don't miss a beat.

There'd be no point trying to get the wipers fixed. Once
when my father came to visit from Victoria, we ended up
having the inevitable discussion about "island time". Dad said
even on Vancouver Island these days you couldn't expect to
get anything done in a hurry. He had taken his radio to an
electrician two weeks ago and he still hadn't got it fixed.
"That's nothing," said my elderly neighbour, Frieda Unsworth.
"I took my car to a mechanic in Masset seven years ago and I
haven't got it back yet."

～～～

Masset's the kind of small town where you recognize everyone by the vehicle they drive, and the Liquor Store employees can tell you what anybody in town drinks and whether they've been drinking too much, lately, for their own good. A trucker I met laughed when I mentioned the Masset Liquor Store must be the only liquor outlet in the world where visitors are asked to sign a guest book as they leave. "Sometimes I sign it twice a day myself," he said. (Comments in the Guest Book range from "excellent liquor" and "Drunk, 7-24-98 10:23 a.m. Wolf Parnell" to "The wine here is cheaper than the gas.")

When people find out where I live they often ask, "Don't you feel isolated, living out there, away from it all?" I even had a taxi driver in Toronto ask me if I came from an "excluded" sort of place.

Living in seclusion, or exclusion if you like, does have advantages. People are forced, by circumstances, to be polite to one another. You can't risk running the local undertaker off the road because he turns in front of you without signalling: you may need his expertise one day. Living in a small town you never have to use your turn signals: everyone knows where you are going, anyway.

In Masset, everybody knows where you've been. They know what you do for a living, and who you are married to — at the moment. For this reason I always try to behave myself when I go to town. I'm especially well-behaved in the post office, because mail is my livelihood — and the last person I want to alienate is the person who sorts my cheques. A friend who got a job sorting mail at Tlell found a registered letter for an island poet, Hibby Gren, who had been dead for ten years. The postmistress, back then, had decided Hibby had been too drunk to be entrusted with important registered mail, so she'd held on to it for fifteen years.

∿∿∿

At the north end of the world, home to any number of social misfits who have fled from the normal stresses of twenty-first century living, the barter system is alive and well. If you want all your garbage hauled away, you leave a reefer on top of your can as an incentive for the local collector. In the old days when they hired strippers at the hotel, one famous North Beach comber is said to have offered an exotic dancer 50 lbs of shrimp to pass the night with him.

Life is simple here, pared down to the bare necessities. There is only one traffic light, for instance, and few other signs giving directions. There is a sign announcing WIGGINS ROAD AHEAD, a few meters before you come to Wiggins Road itself, and that tells you something about the frequency of side roads off the highway connecting Queen Charlotte City with Masset. And then there's the WILDLIFE VIEWING sign underneath the one indicating MASSET CEMETERY ROAD. From what I remember of the people who are now permanent residents in the graveyard, "wild life" viewing would be an understatement.

The graveyard is one of the places I like to spend quiet time, though. The trees drip moss, the graves themselves are overgrown with salal, salmonberry bushes, and more moss. I haven't chosen the precise spot, but one day I expect to take up residence there myself. "Everybody loves that graveyard," said my friend Henry White, as I helped him undecorate his Christmas tree on the Ides of March. "One guy even *hanged* himself in there."

∿∿∿

But the simple life gets busy here. Between cleaning crabs, gutting deer, canning razor clams, and picking huckleberries for pie, I finally find time to finish the article about Yang Zhengxue and the limestone cave dwellers. The only modern appliance they possess is a battery-operated, red plastic alarm clock. Twice a day its owner lets it chirp on and on, for forty-five minutes or more — "not to tell the time, but to entertain, like music from a Stone Age radio."

Those cave dwellers sound too high tech for me, and no place else compares to living where you can see seven rainbows in the sky at once, or count twenty-five eagles perched on the same rock, or lie out under the stars in August and watch the Perseids, the Northern Lights and forked lightning all at the same time. When the storms start howling and the plane doesn't come in, and the ferry is stuck in Prince Rupert and supplies are running low in the Co-Op and the Government Liquor Store, there's no place on this earth I'd rather be.

BEING HERE

I've driven to the ICBC office in Masset to buy insurance for my truck; Irene, who sees me coming, doesn't get the CLOSED sign up fast enough. My insurance expired on Christmas Day, but I haven't received notification from ICBC. "It's probably because I haven't been here," I say, "to check my mail."

Irene asks to see my driver's license. The Sidney, BC address on my license is different from the Masset address on my truck insurance papers.

Irene says I should change the address on my insurance papers if I don't live here, in Masset, at least 330 days out of the year. "My truck lives here," I say, "365 days."

Some wag once said the difference between a comic and a comedian is that the former says funny things and the latter says things funny. There must be a third category for someone like me who can do two things at once: say lots of not funny things in a funny (i.e. not funny) way.

Irene asks if I have been here for more than thirty days. It sounds like a trick question. "What am I supposed to tell you?" I ask, thinking myself quite the card for coming up with a trick response.

"The truth," says Irene.

"I got here last night," I say. I should have left it at that. "But in the summer I was here for more than thirty days."

"Then you should have changed the address on your driver's license," Irene says. She sits down at her computer and begins trying to find me in cyberspace. "The rule is, if you are living here for more than thirty days, you have to change your address."

"How exactly do you define 'living'?" I ask.

She fixes her eyes on the clock above her desk — the big hand has MINUTES written on it, the smaller one HOURS.

"Does 'living' mean that if I am physically here for more than thirty days, I live here?" I ask, determined to sort it out.

"It's not up to me to tell you where you live," Irene says.

That wasn't what I had asked. "I'm not trying to be difficult," I say. "It's just that I have a problem with this. If I am just here for thirty days — I don't live here. But if I am here for more than thirty days, I live here, and I am supposed to change my address."

I interpret her silence as a small but not insignificant victory. She continues her search on the Internet.

"And there's this. At what point does the thirty day period when I'm supposed to live here start? The moment I leave the other place I live or when I arrive on the Island? It took me two days to drive here, so technically I wasn't living at my other address during that time, and I wasn't here, either. I'm not all here and I'm not all there. It's a — grey area."

"I don't care where you live, I'm just telling you," she says, flashing me an annoyed look. I suspect she would like to tell me where to live, or at least where to go. "You bring your license in and I put a change of address sticker on it. That's all there is to it. It's not such a difficult thing."

It's not difficult, but is it — necessary? "And then when I go back — to the other place I live — I take my license to an ICBC office and they — peel the sticker off?"

"That would be common sense," Irene says.

"What if I live in two places?" I am beginning to feel indignant. If anything, a power higher than ICBC should have jurisdiction over my choice of where to live. "Isn't a person allowed to live in more than one place?"

"No one can be in two places at once," Irene replies, now looking annoyed at her computer for not being able to locate me, either. "Not at the same time."

Says who? Just because I have to get on a plane next week and fly my body south doesn't mean the rest of me leaves on the same flight. My imagination, my spirit, live on here, in the house that contains my dreams, on the banks of the Sangan River. In this timeless place, where the ravens speak in tongues as the tides rise and fall, my own life and times begins to make sense to me. What doesn't make sense to me is why, after thirty days, I should have to change the address on my driver's license.

"You-hoo? Hello? How would you like to pay for this?" Irene has found me in the computer, printed the paperwork, and all I have to do is sign, and write a cheque. Then we can both call it quits.

I don't know why I have to push it, but I do. "Say, for the sake of argument, I am homeless. There is nothing to stop a homeless person from owning a car, is there, but if I were homeless, where would I say I lived? I mean, would I have to change my street address every time I moved my car to a different parking spot to avoid getting a ticket? Is this what you're saying?"

That's when Irene looks at me as if to say I am saying a lot of not funny things in a not funny way. I sign the forms.

"Enjoy the rest of your holiday," she says.

These days when I bump into friends they are often in a mighty hurry.

"Great to see you, how you been, how you doing?" the exchange begins, and before I can think of an honest answer, they inevitably reply for me. "Busy?"

Before I can open my mouth to admit, "No, in fact I am not busy, I even had time to schedule half an hour of unscheduled time into my Life-At-A-Glance this morning," they are long gone, cellphone connected importantly to their ear.

Comedian Ellen DeGeneres calls our culture's mad theology of speed TBS (Too Busy Syndrome). Busy implies that life is so harried that we have no time to live it fully. Busy means my phone never stops ringing, with agents calling to offer six figure deals and film moguls scrambling over each other's bodies to option my latest opinion piece. Busy means I have no openings in April or May, but perhaps I can pencil you in for coffee on a slow June Sunday between noon and quarter past.

In her novel, *A Room of One's Own*, Virginia Woolf wrote, "It is in our idleness, in our dreams, that the submerged truth sometimes comes to the top." I have spent much of my life like most of us, leapfrogging from one errand to the next, hurriedly checking off everything on my To Do List before another day grinds to a close. There was little or no time in my overbooked agenda for the kind of dreamy, soulful activities that once upon a time sustained us. Perhaps technology, which forces us to live faster and faster all the time, but not necessarily with any *depth*, can be blamed. Life is about producing — making more money, winning another medal, acquiring more stuff: it's about product nowadays, not process. We have become so obsessed with *doing* that we have nothing left over — time, energy, or imagination — for *being* anymore. Our society values us not for what we are, but for what we do for a living, what we own or strive to acquire. In other words, for our usefulness.

A recent issue of *Utne* addresses our collective conundrum in an article about Mercury Retrograde (a good time, astrologers say, to take a retreat, spend time in solitude, or, at the very least, make our inner life a priority). "The modern world seems to recognize only one pace: busy-ness. Yet for centuries men and women have taught that true contentment lies in the simply lived life, of which unhurried time is a major part." Unhurried time means time to slow down and smell the roses, to take your delight in momentariness, to live for today. We need balance in our lives — to jump when it makes sense to jump (when fleeing to higher ground from a tsunami) and calm down when slowness is called for (waiting for a bed in an Emergency ward). But most people have no time these days to prune the roses let alone slow down long enough to sniff them.

Unhurried time means paying attention to the ant trying to make it from one end of your counter to the other. Taking the best part of a morning to watch a slug going nowhere, slowly. (A friend of mine once stopped traffic on an island bridge because a slug was trying to cross from one side to the other. They whisked him away to the local psychiatric ward;

our culture doesn't have a lot of time for people who come between us and our "getting there".)

A week ago, recovering from a cold and an inner ear infection, I lay in bed listening to what I thought must be ceremonial drumming from the Big House on the nearby reserve. I opened my window to let in more of the sound that has, over the years, connected me with something more time-sacred and transcendent than my ordinary concerns. Silence weighted the night air; when I closed my window the drumming started again, constant, insistent, a heart beat-sound only faster than I'd ever heard it before. This time, I realized, the sound came from inside me, from my own heart racing away in darkness.

I rolled over, trying to escape this persistent reminder of my mortality. My heartbeat only began to slow to its normal comforting pace when I relaxed, breathed deeply, and began really *listening* to it. I had to come to grips with it: my heart, that lonely muscle, wasn't going to go on thumping away inside me forever. Like everything else in this too-busy life, I told myself, it is only temporary.

HOW DO WE KNOW BEAUTY WHEN WE SEE IT: TWENTY MEDITATIONS ON STONES

1. Touchstones

I have never worn precious stones — diamonds in my earlobes, square-cut emeralds on my fingers or sapphires blue as the unappeasable sky. For me, jewels, in their flashiness, are places lonelier than darkness. A beach pebble unadorned, a river rock licked into an egg — the wild, tumbling-free stones — are the ones most precious to me. Stones pulled by tides, polished by the moon; stones like thoughts dealt from the dark; wise stones etched with the faces of burrowing owls; all-seeing stones, alone-stones, holy stones.

There are stones that are markers in my life; touchstones that link me to a place and a time. The green cameo stone from Point-No-Point my lover made into a brooch; the sea-witch's stone, my amulet, from Long Beach on Vancouver Island that I have carried with me since 1969, when it washed up at my feet. The first flowerstone I found on the beach at Metchosin. The chunk of green Connemara marble with a snake slithering through its centre, the agate from Rose Spit with a map of Haida Gwaii indented in it, the river-polished stones from Lawn Creek, copper and bronzed by water falling on cedar, stones that bear the fossilized imprints: a drowned woman's hair, a Mayan warrior's profile. Stones I keep in my pockets for the noise they make rubbing against each other when I have travelled too far away from the sea and can no longer hear its sound. The susurrus of the waves pulling the small stones back into the deep.

Each stone, if it could, would speak of rain and wind, the invisible collisions of kelp, musting bones, and driftwood in the dark. They would say a single grain of sand is as worthy of our praise as the open white flowers of the shining summer plum; that we should beware when too much light falls on everything because if we are blinded by darkness we are also blinded by light.

2. Listening to Stones

Ghandi preached for the self-realization of all living beings. He admitted consulting scorpions and snakes on foreign policy matters.

I listen to stones. They, in their silence, have more to tell me than most people. When I give myself to a stone, I am listening to myself, something older than the present organization of myself.

I have wrapped stones in cedar bark, in leather pouches, in strands of tree moss, in the petals of cauldron-like flowers. As I wrapped, I felt myself being wrapped; I could feel every bruise that may have come to the stone as it was scuttled ashore. What the stone tells me, just through touching: it has nerve-endings, vulnerable parts. A stone changes colour as its moods change. It has a heart, a soul, real eyes to see with. I found a honey-coloured stone that looked like a human brain. I left it on the beach because it was too heavy to carry. A week later I went back to the same spot — a beach with a river running through it, and river-polished stones on either side for miles in each direction. I found the brain-stone again, as if it had been waiting for me. I had help this time, and brought it home.

It seemed to grow lighter the farther inland we drove, and as I climbed out of the truck with it, cradling it as a baby, and set it on the front porch to acclimatize, I noticed it had a soft spot, like a newborn's fontanel. When I touched this spot I felt myself being transported to the other side of consciousness. There I could hear a nurturing stone, a long-lived stone, telling me this: "We come into this world with only the fragile word *I*, an *I* we vainly try braiding into the story of everything else.

3. *Stone markers*

I dreamed of finding a cave where the bodies of the dead had been placed, row upon row, wrapped in cedar bark, with a stone on that part of them which most needed weighing down. For some it was the legs, others the belly, one the groin. One had all seven natural openings of her body closed with stones. Two had stones blocking their ears; three had stones placed on their eyes.

There is no perfect language for describing the emotional state of anyone who feels the sorrow of so many stones; I lifted the stones and set them into a ring in the centre of the cave, and made a fire. At first the stones shrunk away from the flames, but then they began to speak to me in their own language. Even though they'd seen thousands of years of death, they were not unhappy with their lives.

I sat listening to them and when the flames burned down I put them all back where I had found them because I didn't want to interfere. Not with death, or with history, or with the mystery of mysteries. The stones belonged there, in the blackness of the cave. By touching them I felt I had, with my poverty, bought myself a lifetime of days.

4. *Water Over Stones*

I chose the house because of its proximity to the stream. I could lie in bed at night listening to the sound of water sliding heavy over stones. Water slipping around, or underneath them, the lisp and hiss of the silt and gravel being freighted towards the sea. There were nights when that sound was enough, and it was all that I would ever need.

He had enjoyed the stream, too, when he first came to live with me. But after awhile the sound changed, the noise of the water rushing around the stones kept him awake at night, while I slept. Instead of hearing the lullaby of the water over stones, right away in tune with it, his mind would begin to replay a judge's address to the jury, or one of the military marches he'd been forced to listen to as a child.

One day he decided to start moving the rocks in the stream, to see if he could get them to change their tune. If he could just change their pattern, rearrange the stones on the bottom of the creek bed, he felt he could change the sound the water made spilling over them.

This man believed that by altering the world around him he would find peace. I said nothing, other than it would be a big job trying to move some of those boulders that had been there since the last ice age retracted. He laughed and said if he had to he would use dynamite to move them. I felt it was an odd thing to do: blow things up to acquire inner peace, but I had long ago learned not to interfere in other people's search for meaning.

5. *Displaced Stones*

In those inland cities where stones, river rocks chosen for their roundness, are used as decorations — in fountains, in walls or as filler in concrete planter boxes when the flowers have proven too temperamental to live — I feel like a stone out of water, too. I wish I could deliver these stones back to their source, knowing that as they lie here in the fumes, the dust, the gum wrappers and the people going by with Friday on their minds, the stones don't exist, they are in exile.

6. Shape-Shifting Stones

Stones that resemble food: a split baguette, an onion from the downs near Chichester (found on a picnic with Aunt Polly), a perfect beach stone baked potato, the pie-shaped wedge of mica streaked with chocolate brown from the Kiskatinaw River I keep as a paperweight on my desk,
Holy stones: black stones with two white lines intersecting to form a cross, for my mother.
Intifada stones: colourfully painted, softball-sized stones, thrown at Israelis by teenaged Palestinian boys.
Wish stones: flat, soft stones with a hole worn through them. Also called Lucky Stones or (in England) Hag Stones, because they keep witches away.
Fairy stones: stones of weird shape believed to be of supernatural origin and sometimes used as charms.
Lorna's stones: grey or black with a white band of quartz encircling them. Lorna once admired some that Stephen had brought back from the Charlottes, and now neither of us can go anywhere without bringing back at least one of these for Lorna. I don't even know if she really likes them. They pile up in her garden.
Stones that resemble animals: sometimes the shape will call to me from across the beach: "Oh," I hear myself say, "a shark! A turtle." And bears: you need a fat, black, long, oval stone for a bear.

7. *Stones: A Bestiary*

Stones used by shepherds to keep track of the number of animals they had: they collected and kept one pebble for each animal.

Stones used by chimpanzees to crack open nuts placed in depressions in granite outcrops in the Tai forest of the Ivory Coast, Africa.

Stones, a path of stones, as a clue to finding rock wren's (*Salpinctes obsoletus*) stone-sheltered nest.

Stones, a certain rhythmic knocking together of pebbles, used to attract yellow rails (*Coturnicops noveboracensis*).

After the great earthquake in Alaska, fishermen began catching halibut that were full of stones. The fish had felt the tremors and ingested the stones to ballast themselves against the shocks that rocked the ocean floor and reverberated through the currents that bound them. What did the stones feel as they were gulped down into darkness? Did they, like Jonah, have a religious experience?

8. *House of Stone*

"People who live in glass houses shouldn't throw stones," was something my parents often said. I knew there was supposed to be a lesson in this. But what do you do when the house you live in is made of stone? People who live in stone houses, I learned, are made of shatterproof glass.

I collected stones and brought them home, my pockets stretched out of shape from the shapes the stones made settling in against the new curves of my body. I laid them out on the rough wooden bookshelves my father had made. I had packed all my books into boxes and stashed them under my bed, to make room for the stones. Each stone had a story, and

I knew, if I was patient enough, that story would be told to me.

The white pebbles, though, I kept in a different place, remembering another lesson from a book: two children taken into the woods and left there because their father couldn't afford to keep them. Hansel and Gretel leaving a trail of white stones that shone in the moonlight and guided them home. I hid my white stones, smooth and cool as the peppermints I would place under my tongue to make them last, believing, back then, that these white pebbles might one day be the path back to myself.

I had stones the colour of bruises; I had lilac-coloured stones. I had stones orange as California poppies; stones the red of the heroin-blood mix. Edible-looking colours: eggplant, persimmon, watery grape. Stones the colour of licked bones; teeth-shaped stones. I had every shade of green, from the black-green of a fairy-tale forest to the wistful green of a beech grove in early spring. Once I found a heart-shaped stone, small as a black-eyed pea, and just as hard; I lost it before I could find a home for it on one of my shelves. I had triboluminescent stones — ones that give off light if you rub, crush or break them.

Some stones had messages etched into them; others had secrets I never could decipher. Some were like miniature land masses, veined with rivers, crusted with mountains, pink, vermilion, burnt sienna. When the stones grew dull I dipped them in water or coated them with a thin layer of oil I had first warmed in my hands — so that they might always shine. I took cold wet river stones and made them into a cairn on a dry pebble beach. I took stones pocked with the spitting of rain and laid them to dry under a slate-white sky. I made myself a pillow of stone, having grown to believe a stone can be a softer pillow than one made of down; in it I could hear the dense heartbeat of the earth. I slept, but each night a slow *splashing splashing* woke me. My tears, hard rain. One stone knows what another stone is crying about.

9. Carved in Stone

Neglect is a stone in a dead man's house. Stones learn by going where they have to go. Stones have no feet but they get there. Stone flies up where your foot was going. Kick the stone, break your foot. Stone only cries when you pick it up. Who looks at a stone to see a stone. Stone flies like a handkerchief, lands like a sack. Gone like a stone in a river. Buried stone is still a stone. Even a stone goes its own way. Get rid of one stone, end up with two. Not big but a stone. Stone parched by the sun, pants at the moon. Quiet as a stone watching a hole over water. No rust on a stone. Listen even to a stone. Ask the mouth, it says: stone. Stone in both hands: what next. Stone tea better than hell soup. Find a stone in the noodles, lose it in the bath.

10. Stone-Blind Love

What does a stone see as you hold it in your hands?
Who looks at a mirror to see a mirror?
The stone itself is a means to an end, not the end itself.

11. A stone by any other name is still . . .

The English language is bereft of words for stone. We have rock and stone, both of which, by rock-hounds (those who hunt stones, tapping on them with little hammers in the hopes of finding beauty buried inside) are often referred to as *specimens*. In Asian cultures, stone has as many meanings as the word *snow* has for the Inuit peoples of Canada's north.

40 words for stone, from the Korean:
Stones found along the sea or on beaches
Stone with surface resembling an oriental pear
Stone that resembles a rock on the mountain
A single mountain-peak stone
A stone with a shelter or overhang
A large stone
A step stone, or a stone having two or more level plains
A pond stone
A stone that resembles an island
A stone that has a cave
A stone with a pattern resembling flowers
A stone that is curious or grotesque, with multiple
        perforations or creases
Stones resembling animal bones
Stones resembling a turtle's shell, with white inclusions
Stones found in rivers
A stone that resembles a lake
Stones resembling human beings
Stones that resemble animals
A stone that resembles Buddha
A house-shaped stone
Stones of high quality
Stones of a light colour that look like close views of
        mountains
A stone with inclusions resembling Chinese calligraphic
        characters
A stone that resembles a small spring found on mountain
        sides
A stone that has inclusions of white resembling a waterfall
Plains stone: displays a level plain with a mountain or hill
        on the far side of the view

Mountain view stone
Stones found in and around mountains
A double-peak or two mountain stone
Decorative stone
Young stones (those newly collected)
Natural stone: one appreciated for its intrinsic value
Long-lived stone
Nurturing stone
Nourishment of a young stone to make it look older by
watering, hand-rubbing and exposure to the sun
Oriental dragon stone
Mountain range stone (with three or more peaks resembling
        a series of mountains)
Masterpiece Stones
Garden stones
Beautiful Stones

12. Beautiful Stones

I have planted over the years a garden of flowerstones — night-black, some smooth, some jagged — with an alphabet of stars that spell out what it means to be lonely. It is hard to be lonely when you stand in that garden of stones, picking magnolia blossoms from where they have fallen, in the spaces between stars.

Trying to decide where a particular flowerstone should go — in the rock garden or in my shrine next to the ginger pot Stephen made me, beside the eagle skull from Skedans, or the doll wrapped in remnants of grave cloth from Bucaramunga? I decide to take it back to the beach where I found it. That's when I begin to see: other stones that I have overlooked because I was too busy looking for what I clearly expected to find.

Agates are the worst offenders, how they distract me from looking for other stones, trick me by their semi-precious importance. When I bring a handful of agates home, I feel I have been deceived. How can a stone be so beautiful it takes away my eyes?

Holding a single flowerstone in the palm of my hand, always this question: *how do we know beauty when we see it?*

13: Shades of Grey Stones

Break break break/ On thy cold grey stones, O Sea! A cold grey stone can hoard more mysteries than one in which the light shines through.

I have cleanly broken pebbles, grey as first light on a west coast morning. Flat stones grey as old bed sheets. Cracked stones the pale grey of a bitter man's face in a mirror. Steely grey like pigeon feathers, pale grey, the grey of ordinary things, grey like pond-bottom mud. Grey as the powder-covered moth, an oxeye daisy in a roadside ditch. Even bright grey on days when the sun breaks through, smashing the mist with its clenched fist.

14. "There are no blue stones."

A poet writes, "A child will trade a blue river rock for a stick of chewing gum."

Another poet responds: "There are no blue stones."

15. Sacred Stones and Profane

East is East: Suiseki (Sui=water, Seki=stone) is the Japanese name for the "viewing stones", unaltered naturally formed stones found in mountain streams, on deserts, along ocean beaches frequently displayed at Bonsai exhibitions. They are chosen for their perceived resemblance to familiar scenes in nature or to objects closely associated with the natural world. The essence of Suiseki: "The contemplation of a stone as a symbol of nature relaxes the mind from pressures of a complex daily life and allows a person to retain his sense of values. The importance of life in its simplest form is reflected through the beauty, strength and character of the stone."

And West is West: My friend Helen and I found "pet rocks" in a gift shop in Queen Charlotte City: a row of small rocks with cartoon-human faces, glued onto the "bodies" of larger ones. Some had been given hats — jaunty sunhats, baseball caps — or made to smoke cigars made of long thin turret shells. All of them looked like hopeless middle-class tourists: if there is anything on earth less dignified than a human being on vacation, it is two stones crazy-glued together meant to portray a human being on vacation.

Helen and I decapitated one of these hostage-rocks every time we went to the shop, and released the garishly painted heads back into the sea. We kept up our good work until only a row of dumpy rocks with yellow neckties and red-checked halter suntops remained, apparently unnoticed, squatting headless on a dusty shelf. Over the next months we carried what was left of the body parts down to the sea, and committed them to the depths, knowing they would survive. When you've lived once, they say, you never forget how.

And never the twain shall meet: From an item in Maine Rock Designs catalogue. "Stimulate conversation and recall quiet walks on the beach with these unique accessories for the bar and kitchen. Where else could you find a *Sheffield cheese knife set in a 390 million year-old hand-polished stone?*

16. Two More Facets of Stone

Stones, seven of them, found at an archaeological site in Syria, an early set of weights used during the Stone Age.

Stones used to hold down leaves placed as "lids" on top of fermented breadfruit stored in stone-lined pits in Tahiti.

17. Healing Stones

Massage therapists place stones (well-rounded cobbles) treated with hot lavender oil on a client's head, chest, abdomen, and hips. Thumb-sized pebbles are placed between adjacent toes. "Toe treatment helps the client connect with nature."

Hot stone therapy was used thousands of years ago by the Chinese to treat rheumatism and by Native Americans in sweat lodges. It was also used during the Spanish Inquisition, but to a different end: hot stones were placed between a client's toes to torture him.

18. Rebel Stones

A rusty sign on a pole near the border with Northern Ireland warning, in both English and Irish: "Persons throwing stones at the telegraph will be prosecuted."

19. Ritual Stones

Small pebbles make up the moving parts of rainsticks, used in ceremonies to bring rain to the world's desert regions. Whenever the "sticks" (branches of Quiso cacti filled with the pebbles, and their ends sealed) are tipped over they emit a sound resembling a sprinkling of rain building to the swoosh of a tropical downpour.

During their initiation ceremonies, believers in Santeria (saint worship) use vessels made of china and wood containing smooth stones in which the spirits of the gods reside.

The Nenets, a nomadic tribe of reindeer herders of the Siberian Arctic, believe that certain stones are remnants of the gods who have guarded them for millennia.

20. Heart of Stone

I hold my amulet in the palm of my hand, watching it change colour, watching for new faces and symbols to emerge. Sometimes a whale with whiskers appears, a dancing sea-horse, a question mark, a star. If I hold the stone to my ear I can hear more than just the faraway sound of the sea; I hear fields of croaking frogs, clouds blowing from the hills, ice breaking up in the well behind the house, a cat with grey eyes howling beside the cabin wall.

What does the stone see as it rests in the palm of my hand? It sees the tiny ridges on my fingertips, a swirling weather system of loops, arches and whorls, the distinct signature I imprint upon it, which, like tracks left behind through the silver-grey stones of tundra, can last a thousand years.

I found this stone more than thirty years ago and it has travelled with me ever since in a leather pouch that has been worn shiny and smooth from so much touching. Every time I return to the west coast I dip it in the ocean so that its energy can be renewed. I always go alone. Sometimes I expect a wave, waiting for me to make a simple mistake of venturing out too far into the deceptive water, to snatch the stone from me. How many winters has this stone been host to the moon and its light, even while I keep it wrapped up, in the leather pouch I am never without, in darkness?

I wish to be buried, one day, with this stone in my hand. I hold it in my palm and I imagine my flesh spirited away, my finger bones curling around the stone, and the warmth it will bring me, pulled from the stars.

HEROIN CHRISTMAS

The Personal

"We're not here right now. Leave a message." Please, I add for them. And hang up the phone.

I drive my daughter's friends home. Not one utters "thank you" as they slouch from the car. I try to keep in mind what one etiquette expert wrote: "We are all born charming, fresh and spontaneous and must be civilized before we are fit to participate in society."

Rudeness, or "the absence of the sacrament of consideration," is endemic — another by-product of our spiritually impoverished society. Wouldn't the world be a more hospitable place if people just said "please" and "thank you" a little more often?

A business associate's new dog snaps at me as I step over his body to get out the door. "Oh," says his owner, "he's never done that before." No doubt this accusation (i.e. there must be something about me the dog senses that nobody else does) is uttered out of embarrassment, but a simple "I'm sorry" would have more than paid for the new hole in my tights.

In the drugstore a woman pays for her purchases while yaking in a foreign (to me) tongue on her cellphone; the person serving her might as well be a pile of dog excrement for all the courtesy being extended to her. The cellphone is one more way in which we have become separated from connectedness to one another. (Call Waiting is another monumental threat to civility: how rude can a person be to put you on hold in case another, more important, caller is waiting?)

"Manners maketh man" was my father's favourite maxim. He grew up in a time when a gentleman, faultlessly gloved, could not go far wrong. And it was considered a sign of ill-breeding for a lady to go up the stairs of a hotel humming a tune — "it may expose her to rudeness". The last time I stayed in a hotel (an upscale hotel in downtown Toronto) I don't recall humming in the elevator but just after midnight a gentleman (undeniably ungloved) began pounding on my door demanding that someone named Fuckface "Open up." The animals in our country have better manners than some human beings.

The marks of a sick culture, says novelist Robert Heinlein, include everything from particularism (identifying one's self with a particular group, religion, race or language, rather than with the population as a whole); male domination; loss of faith in the justice system; high taxation; inflation; and violence. A dying culture, however, exhibits personal rudeness. "Bad manners. Lack of consideration for others in minor matters."

The key words here are " minor matters". One would hardly declare America rude for bombing Iraq and killing civilians for world peace and oil, though in some civilized circles this might be considered, among other things, extremely Non-U. But the young woman who leaves a message on her sociology prof's answering machine, "You fat fuck with yellow teeth! You hump!" (her problem? she couldn't resell her textbook), or the young man who brings his portable television into a Grade Nine classroom and, when asked to turn if off, grabs his genitals and pumps his hand up and down, are examples of widespread rudeness and a decaying

SUSAN MUSGRAVE

culture in which many individuals now place their own comfort ahead of the comfort, and even the safety, of others.

A rude encounter is remembered for a lifetime. An elderly friend tells me how her life has changed since her husband was killed in a car accident. Driving herself to the shops for the first time, she hesitated before merging onto the main road; a young woman pulled out from behind her, shouting, "You die, Wrinkles!" Florence said she took the car home, parked it, and hasn't gone out since.

"Highway discourtesy and the perception of being treated disrespectfully are also now commonplace motives for crime," Judith Martin points out in her *Miss Manners* column. "Whether they realize it or not, aggressive drivers and touchy teenagers care so much about etiquette that they will kill to maintain it."

Drivers who hog the passing lane take note: it is extremely discourteous, even though you may be driving the speed limit and therefore feel entitled to stay put, not to move over to let others pass. In some cases such behaviour can be deadly: one must keep in mind Miss Manner's admonition, however, that killing is not the approved method for keeping society polite.

Etiquette is important in human interactions because it is a matter of showing dignity for human nature itself. To be treated politely is a fundamental need — perhaps even a human right. So please, let's unlearn our new-found common rudeness and return to common courtesy. Thank you. Very much.

THE DYING ART OF TENT RAISING

When I was a child I dreamed of going camping. My father didn't believe in that kind of suffering. He said being cooped up in a leaky tent with four kids and my mother in the rain was his idea of living hell. Instead we all went out on his boat. Four of us and my mother all cooped up down below while my father, up above in his sou'wester, tried to caulk the seams in the decks that leaked when it rained, which it did every summer.

Last year our own children begged us to take them camping. Camping was cool. They'd seen it on TV. Besides, we'd be together all day as a family in the car, getting there. And, since Dad couldn't smoke in the car, he could use the opportunity to quit smoking, just like he'd been threatening to.

The first day was pretty standard, the kids fighting over who got to sit in the front seat, all of us fighting over whose turn it was to listen to Kurt Cobain, Raffi or Pavarotti. We ended up compromising on "Found a Peanut".

Despair didn't set in until we approached Hope. It had been close in the car but as soon as we hit the national park the first clouds rolled in over the mountains. As I rolled the sleeping bags out to air, the first raindrops began to settle the dust that was making my eldest daughter have asthma.

On either side of us, vacationers were pulling up in their RVs, setting up their satellite dishes and microwaving dinner, while I was trying to find matches to get a pile of wet cedar burning into some kind of smudge fire to suffocate the mosquitoes, and my husband was giving the children a lecture on the dying art of tent raising.

If you set up a tent in a provincial campsite these days you become another roadside attraction. People drive out from the nearest town to ogle you, the RCMP cruise past and make a note of your license plate number. One couple stopped their Winnebago in front of our site and asked if they could be photographed beside our tent "for old time's sake". They'd got married in 1932 and gone on a tenting honeymoon. The husband said, "We soon grew out of that phase though. That's why we've stayed married."

The kids, tired from fighting in the car all day, demanded Smurfaghetti. I never lower my standards just because I'm roughing it: on tonight's menu was Freeze-Dried Gourmet Style Beans. The word "style" should have been a tip-off — all you had to do, once you got the fire blazing, was add water. Of course the nearest tap was half a mile down the road by the outhouse the kids wouldn't venture near because it smelled "different" from our bathroom at home.

But by now the rain was washing out the fire pit so I gave up trying to cook. We drove ten miles back down the road to eat at a family restaurant. I told my husband that if he said, "Are we having fun yet?" one more time, I was leaving him. It turned out I couldn't have left even if I'd wanted to because my husband had absentmindedly locked the keys in the car. I had to call the Canadian Automobile Association's 1-800 number and ask them to send someone capable of breaking into our car.

The next night we attended a lecture on bears. The ranger told us never to keep shampoo, deodorant, or toothpaste in our tent because bears are attracted to the perfumed scent. Lock your toiletries in the trunk of the car, he cautioned us. If you want to discourage bears, the natural state of unwashed human flesh is the best deterrent.

By the end of the lecture I was considering locking myself in the car. But when we got back to the campsite my husband had absentmindedly locked the keys in the trunk of the car and, after calling the Automobile Association again — who said they'd send a truck in the morning — I crawled into my sleeping bag along with our toiletries, with the vain hope a bear wouldn't be attracted to them if they were in the same bag as my unwashed feet. My husband stayed up late making twig tea on the fire. He'd read that it helped curb nicotine cravings.

On the last day of our vacation my husband lost the car keys altogether. I accused him of absentmindedly losing his mind and called the CAA. "Don't tell me, let me guess," the dispatcher interrupted when I began to explain. "Your name is Susan Musgrave and you're locked out of your car again."

On our way home we decided not to camp but to drop in on some friends who had a cottage on Larvae Lake. We all needed baths — no human beings had come near us for days, let alone bears. I was too demoralized to cook, so we stopped to pick up a can of Smurfaghetti for the kids and a package of Player's Light for my husband.

Our friends were throwing a barbecue. One of their guests had a child who demanded Smurfaghetti because my kids were having it. Her mother said no dear we don't eat that kind of food. My husband was chain smoking on the balcony so I slunk into a corner with some escapist literature I'd brought with me for the camping trip: *Pain and Possibility: Making the*

Most out of Personal Crisis. This was the first time on our holiday I'd had time to read a book.

Relaxing, I had just read, was a major cause of stress — when the mother (who must have felt guilty for sounding judgemental) tried to strike up a conversation. She asked me if I was reading *Pain and Possibility* for pleasure. I said it depends, and she looked at me in a new way. "What's your last name?" she said.

I told her. After a stunned pause, she asked, "Are you *the* Susan Musgrave."

For a terrible moment I thought she must work for the CAA. She's the dispatcher I've spoken to every time I dialled that 1-800 number. Then she said, "I studied your poetry at university." And added, superfluously I thought, "You don't look anything like your poetry."

Before I could tell her that was because I'd been relaxing for two weeks, her husband, who had been eavesdropping, chimed in. He guessed I must be *the* Susan Musgrave married to the Jim Musgrave who had the Massey-Ferguson franchise up the road. In any case I'm sure their daughter now gets Smurfaghetti on demand.

Next year our family is going to find out what suffering is *really* all about. My husband has decided to buy a boat — so I can look forward to a second childhood.

MOTHER'S DAY IN IRELAND

My father used to say, "Every day is Mother's Day." I suspect, now, this was his way of not having to spend money on a gift, and when I had children of my own I found myself repeating the same words, knowing how true, and also how wrong, he was. When my eldest daughter was ten, I asked her what Mother's Day meant to her. "It's the day your mother is supposed to do something special for you," she said.

I thought so.

On our third night in Ireland, while my mother and I waited for a table in the dining room, I asked a man, who looked like he might have had a mother once, if they celebrated Mother's Day in this country. He stared deeply into his drink, and then said, "I'd say we do. Back in March, was it?" He looked at his partner for backup.

"In March. The 17th, I'd say, for sure," the man continued, then launched into a song about his dear old mother being dead and in her grave, at a mighty volume.

"If he carried on like that at home," my mother says, "he would be quietly escorted out."

My mother and I have been here before. At some point on our holiday, she invariably says *I always have such a lovely time in Ireland. It's so sad to think I will never see it again.* Mum's last trip to Ireland has become an annual event — like growing older.

The first time she said she would never see Ireland again I figured she must be prescient. After two weeks of driving down the wrong side of roads narrower than bicycle paths at home, with her in the passenger seat sucking air through her teeth going *sssst sssst sssst* every time I grazed a stone wall or sideswiped a pedestrian, I confess that murder had crossed my mind. But as I've aged, too, I have learned to be more accepting of those things I cannot change in either my mother (her tendency to worry) or myself (my tendency to worry that I am starting to worry too much like my mother).

Her new worry is that her luggage looks the same as everybody else's. My young daughter helps her choose a sticker that will distinguish her bag from the rest: it says BOMB ON BOARD. In the end she buys a roll of tape and covers her black bag with red crosses reminiscent of a Swiss doctor's kit. Why, I wonder, couldn't she have stuck a Happy Face decal on her suitcase, like everybody else's mother?

Because she's *my* mother, that's why. And it's why I love her. She has a mind of her own, and a suitcase like nobody else's, also.

On our last sojourn to the old sod, we climbed the Hill of Tara, mythical home of gods and heroes since the Stone Age, and former seat of the High Kings of Ireland. My mother took a picture of me sitting amongst sheep on the Mound of the Hostages, then left me to think lofty thoughts while she explored the small converted church of St. Patrick and its adjacent churchyard, looking for, she confessed later, the stone bearing "a rude carving" a signpost had warned us about. She never found it, and this year we made a special trip to look again, only to find the gates locked and the hills barred due to Foot and Mouth Disease.

From the moment we stepped off the plane in Dublin and walked through the first of many disinfected carpets, we were constantly reminded of our potential, as visitors to the country, to contaminate.

"How long will you be staying in Ireland?" the ruddy-faced immigration officer asked as I presented my passport and landing card. My mother had already passed inspection and was waiting for me up ahead.

"A couple of weeks," I said.

"How long might that be — three, four, the rest of your life?" he continued. "In Ireland a couple of weeks can mean anything. You could be planning on staying long enough to start pushing up daisies."

"Two weeks," I said, glancing at my mother who was taking down the phone number of a Good Samaritan organization from a poster. "ANXIOUS? DEPRESSED? SUICIDAL? WE'RE THERE AND WE CARE." This reminded me: my mother had recently quit smoking to save money to pay for our holiday. "Fifteen days, to be exact," I added. "If one of us doesn't strangle the other one first."

"Travelling with your mother, is it?" he asked, finally stamping my passport. He told me to have a grand time and to behave ourselves whatever else we got up to.

I assured him we would. We have all kinds of adventures, my mother and I, some of which I will never live down. Last time it was the pothole — the first day. I blamed it on jet lag, and not seeing the sign saying DAMAGED ROAD AHEAD, but she insisted I'd had a choice. The choice, I argued, was a head-on collision with a forty-foot lorry marked DANGER EXPLOSIVES, or the eight inch-deep pothole (my mother measured it): I opted, sensibly, I'd thought, for the pothole. This year it was booking us into the "charming old-world hotel" I'd found on the Internet.

I suspect my mother had been hoping for something more welcoming, like the proverbial red carpet found outside most high class hotels and not the ratty piece of foam mattress saturated with disinfectant we had to walk through to get to the front door of the High Class Hotel. The proprietor looked suspicious when we inquired about three nights accommodation; I got the feeling he was more accustomed to renting rooms by the hour.

I hauled our suitcases up the stairs, unlocked my door, and tried not to get hypnotized by the carpet that looked as if a previous occupant had washed down a six course Mexican meal with a bottle of Southern Comfort, and doodled crude imitations of Megalithic art in the ensuing vomit. I arranged myself around the bedsprings on the sagging mattress, inserted my ear-plugs, and tried to sleep.

There was, alas, no rest for my mother, whose room over the generator, she said, made her so nostalgic for the sound of the jet engine we'd left behind on the runway in Dublin, that she wanted to fly home immediately. When her kettle refused to boil it was the last straw — she reached for her telephone to call the Samaritans, but her phone was out of order.

"Look at it this way," I said, trying to save face, and my inheritance. "The price was right. You'll have enough money left over to buy duty-free cigarettes." I didn't add that I had also given her something new to hold against me, if she ever got tired of the pothole.

My mother agreed to accompany me to the Tourist Office to see if there was anywhere else she might prefer to spend the rest of our holiday. The kindly woman at Bord Failte recommended a hotel that had recently been converted from a railway station. "It's absolutely nice," she assured my mother. "I've had dinner there myself several times, and I've never yet been poisoned."

We were desperate enough to take her recommendation, and the place turned out to be much nicer than nice. My room, the Bridal Suite, had a four-poster bed, linen sheets, and a mattress that was absolutely virginal compared with the one I'd failed to fall asleep on at the High Class Hotel.

Thirty years ago — the year I turned twenty — I spent the winter in a cottage on the west coast of Ireland, two miles from the small town of Ballyconneely and about ten miles from Clifden. My mother came to visit me in early June. I couldn't afford a car in those days, and hitch-hiked into Clifden once a week to take a bath at the Celtic Hotel in exchange for doing some typing for the owner. My mother had to hitch-hike with me; she will never forget getting a ride into town with the priest the first day, and back home again with the doctor, and how Mrs. O'Sullivan at the post office said it was normally the other way around — you came in with the doctor and went out with the priest.

My mother took a room at the Red Cottage, where Rita O'Neill put the cabbage on to boil, for dinner, the moment she'd finished washing the breakfast dishes. We ate her boiled cabbage and mackerel, once. After that we invented relatives — a new one every night — who had kindly invited us for a meal, we said.

Valentine Early, my toothless neighbour, who was then well into his eighties, took a shine to my mother. "Have ye a husband?" Val asked her, after I made introductions. My mother said yes; I added that my father was back in Canada. This didn't slow Val down. "Has he his health?" he asked my mum.

Now, every year we do the same thing, more or less. We spend two weeks touring and worrying, then fly home and thrive for another year on memories: of Gort, near Yeat's Tower; Thoor Ballylee, where I buy gum boots made from Dunlop tires; of drinking seaweed-tasting tea at the same teahouse in Roundstone; of buying sweaters, hand-knitted in Donegal, in Clifden; of stopping to take a picture of a ruin — "her castle" is how my mother has come to think of it — on a tiny island in the middle of a lake near Ballynahinch.

This year we did something different. We visited Newgrange, a 5000 year-old Neolithic mound covering a prehistoric passage tomb. Before entering the tomb our guide warned us that it could get extremely close inside: anyone with a fear of tight spots should stick to the rear in case they needed to exit fast. We squeezed in, single file, and stood preparing to watch a simulated light show (what visitors to Newgrange would see if they stood in the chamber at dawn on the morning of the winter solstice — a shaft of sunlight penetrating the passage, creeping slowly to the very back of the chamber).

When the lights went out I whispered to my mother, was she feeling claustrophobic yet?

My mother laughed and said the burial chamber was far more commodious than her room at that hotel I'd booked over the Internet.

On Mother's Day, this year, I can't be home with my daughters. I won't be able to do anything special for them, except love them, unconditionally, from afar. I'll be driving down some damaged road with my mother who will say, at some point along the way, *I always have such a lovely time in Ireland. It's so sad to think I'll never see it again.* So I vow to make every day we have here my mother's day, for as long as our journey lasts.

THE BEST FAMILIES

Last week I wrote my mother a thank-you letter. I thanked her for being understanding when my teenaged daughter loaned my car to friends who drove it in first gear and burned the engine out. I thanked her for paying for the rebuilt engine instead of saying, "it's payback time". I thanked her for taking me shopping to buy a new outfit to wear when I had lunch with the Queen (two days after the event I discovered the price tag dangling from the armpit of my faux-fur coat). But most of all I thanked her for giving birth to me when she was young, so that she is still here for me in the years when I appreciate her and need her most.

After lunching with the Royals (my mother worries I made the guest list because I helped rewrite the Oath of Canadian Citizenship years ago and suggested the Queen be axed), I took a detour by the family home to thank her for teaching me good manners ("Imagine you're having lunch with the Queen" was the line I most often heard at mealtimes when I was growing up) and to let her know Her Majesty envied my smart new "afternoon dress". I could tell by the way she looked right through me.

"I was afraid to open your letter," my mother said, which, in my excitement at brushing with greatness, I had forgotten I had sent. "I thought you were writing to tell me you wished you had a different mother. You didn't mention coming to

Long Beach for Thanksgiving, either. You probably have something more important to do."

Mum says the same thing every year before six carloads full of family prepare to make the six-hour journey to Tofino. Of course I still plan on driving her. I say; yes, I'll have my tires rotated if she promises she won't spend the whole time worrying about my emergency brake she's convinced is due to fail.

By mistake, this year, my mother watched a television program about old folks in the States being wheeled to shopping malls by their adult children, and abandoned there. Some were fighting back by having computerized chips surgically implanted under their skin so that when they are found they will be able to be identified. I assure my mother I have no plans to dump her on the Long Beach Road at the side of Sproat Lake, but when I offer to help pack her First Aid kit for our trip ("accidents will occur even in the best families") I can't help but notice she's written her name and Social Security number in permanent marker on her arm. "That's for when your car goes off the cliff. How else will they be able to identify my body?"

Happiness, George Burns said, is having a large, loving, caring, close-knit family in another city. My family all live within striking distance on the same island, which means no one gets stuck with a long-distance phone bill when it comes time to planning the annual Thanksgiving meal.

There was the year we had to boycott turkey because a nephew came home from elementary school with a Wild About Turkey Education box and an assignment to raise turkey-consciousness in the weeks leading up to Thanksgiving. Last year a niece threatened to go on a hunger strike to protest "the wholesale slaughter of turkeys", and we stuffed a vegetable marrow instead. I'm by far the easiest one to please: I'll eat turkey, as long as it's organic.

My brother, the negotiator, suggests that this year we roast a salmon on the beach. The side of the family that bears WILD SALMON DON'T DO DRUGS bumper stickers says, only if he catches a sockeye himself, because eating a farmed salmon would be tantamount to eating an eighty-year-old cancer patient.

Heeding my mother's advice, that accidents will happen, I take my car to have the tires rotated and the emergency brake greased. Thanksgiving wouldn't be the same if my car went off the cliff and she wasn't here, next year, to say, "You didn't mention coming to Long Beach for Thanksgiving. You probably have something more important to do."

GETTING IN THE SPIT-IT

I grew up thinking Jesus Christ was a swear word. In a family crisis, like when our old boat's engine cut out, or when the mast snapped in the midst of a southeast gale, my father would frequently take the Lord's name in vain.

Because boating was my father's religion, I missed out on experiences like Sunday School. I remember quizzing a friend — what exactly went on behind those closed church doors? I felt I might be missing something.

"We study Jesus Christ," she said.

I was impressed. "They get to study a swear word," I told my mum.

That year my mother decided I needed some religious instruction, and took me to a midnight carol service on Christmas Eve. What I remember most, besides my mother praying for a hurricane so we wouldn't have to go boating during the holiday season, was the way the Anglican minister burred and clipped his 'r's, so that "spirrrit" became "spit-it", as in the Spit-It of Christmas.

Church was a departure from our family tradition, our unique way of getting in the Spit-it. On Christmas Eve we'd usually pile into my father's old Buick and go for a drive to look at the coloured lights and what my daughter now refers to as "negativity scenes." Each year, without fail, my father reminded us that Jesus had chosen to be born in a subtropical desert where it never snowed. How was it, he wanted to know, that snow had become the universal symbol of the Nativity? My mother would deeply sigh, by way of an answer.

Our drive-by led over the Johnson Street Bridge, where my father would point out where the homeless would be celebrating Christmas, and on past the orphanage, as if to further remind us (I believed) how much we had to be grateful for. Santa couldn't leave presents for the orphans because their roof was too steep for his eight tiny reindeer.

The Christmas cards I choose for my family and friends depict a lifelong preoccupation with childhood's unfinished business. One features Rudolph the Nasally-Challenged reindeer plopped down in an overstuffed armchair, reading "The Christmas Carol", his rifle propped against the wall. Above him, mounted like trophies, are the heads of all the other reindeer, from Dasher on down to Donner and Blitzen. "All of the other reindeer used to laugh and call him names," the caption says.

My favourite, what I call the Orphan's Revenge, shows an overstuffed Santa seated before a small pile of gnawed bones and antlers. The words "Ate tiny reindeer" are written above his head.

In the dark days of December leading up to J.C's birth, my sense of humour becomes an even darker shade of black. When I buy rat poison at the hardware store and the clerk, humorously wearing antlers on her head, says, "Have an awesome Christmas," I want to tell her, "I have other plans." When I buy roofing tar to patch the spot where it is dripping over the Christmas tree, threatening to short out the lights, and the salesgirl says, "at least you have a roof, think of the homeless people under the Johnson Street Bridge"; I consider the advantages to jumping *off* a bridge. When I spend my Christmas nest-egg on a cocktail of pharmaceuticals and the winking pharmacist says, "Have a better than good Christmas!" I'm tempted, like the Anglican minister, to hiss "Spit-it!" And when I return to my car and the commissioner issuing me a ticket for parking more than three feet from the artificial Christmas tree on the curb, wishes me a safe holiday, I am tempted to swear, "Jesus Christ, why don't you wish me a Belated 9/11 while you're at it?"

My daughter, whose last year's letter to Santa Claus (which begins "Dear Sanity Clause") contained a bomb threat ("If I don't get the butane lighter you promised me the chimney goes ka-boom"), has discovered an Internet site selling heavenly relics. For the person who has everything, there's Jesus the Hot Air Balloon — 110 feet high, weighing more than 750 pounds and containing 258,000 cubic feet of sanctified air (no price listed) — and for the kids, a Baby Jesus Paddleball game. You can order your Christmas gifts wrapped, in glow-in-the-dark paper depicting, what else? A negativity scene.

THE GIFTS WE BEAR

The first gifts have arrived from the east: socks, mittens and toques for everyone in the family, knitted by Grandma Susie. I wear her cherished socks to my office each day (I get cold feet, writing) and a toque — to keep the heat, and my thoughts, from escaping through the top of my head. When my fingers start to freeze, I'm tempted to slip on a pair of mittens — but it's too hard to type that way. While I work, putting one word in front of another, I think of Grandma's tireless hands, all the small stitches she put into a life, one at a time.

These gifts last forever — the priceless ones: the album my mother composed (photographs of my father, drenched in dead light); the year my daughter had five dollars to her name and went to the flea market to buy my gifts (a belt made for a Barbie doll's waist and a pullover made for a Buddha); the Christmas my husband went all out and bought me the Power Book I couldn't afford (which, when the bill came in, I secretly paid for, knowing he could afford it even less). For me it has always been easier to give, to lighten my own load rather than bear the weight of other people's caring.

Sometimes, though, giving can get to be too much. Having to buy a pop-up hot dog cooker for a sister-in-law you never see because three wise men bearing gifts to the Babe in the manger invented the custom of giving Christmas presents centuries ago, is a terrible thing. Consumption being sacred, we continue to search for "the perfect gift", the one that says "I love you" with a price tag that shows how much. We celebrate the birth of a very wise man who said we should give all we have to the poor by showering each other with ultrasonic jewellery cleaners and motorized tie racks.

"Forgive me, giver, if I destroy the gift. It is so nearly what I would have wished for, I could not help but perfect it," wrote the American poet, Laura Riding. A noble sentiment, in theory, but most days I don't consider destroying my Power Book in order to perfect it; I am still, in part, a material girl. Besides, as my mother would say, to trash my laptop would be looking a gift horse in the mouth.

Last night I re-read "The Gift of the Magi", a tale about the rewards of unselfish love, to my daughter, hoping she would understand why Santa will be making a donation, in her name, to the orphans of Afghanistan this Christmas and why she won't be getting the butane lighter on her list. In O. Henry's story, a woman sells her long beautiful locks to get enough money to buy a Christmas gift for her husband: a platinum fob chain for his prized gold watch. Her husband, meanwhile, is downtown hawking his watch to buy the set of tortoise shell combs his wife had worshipped in a shop window — for her hair.

"These two unwisely sacrificed for each other the greatest treasures of their house," O. Henry writes. "But let it be said . . . that of all who give and receive gifts, such as they, are wisest."

My father, a wise man in his way, refused to go into debt over Christmas. Coloured lights were a waste of electricity, wrapping paper a waste of trees. "Christmas is about family," he would say, much to my horror. I didn't want togetherness; I wanted gifts. Things you could touch.

The one gift I have left that my father gave me — the one, that is, I can still touch — is the charm bracelet he bought on a trip to South Africa. I often hold it in my hands — the bracelet I never wore — and think of him standing in some shop, in a foreign land, trying to decide which souvenir would appeal to me most, the daughter he tried to know.

Grandma Susie died last May. She was still young, her hands not ready to let slip the beautiful and comforting things they made. "That means we won't be getting any more socks this year for Christmas!" my daughter cried, when I had to break the news.

But Grandma had finished this year's Christmas knitting in the long dark evenings before spring, as if she understood the importance of continuing to give, long after it was expected of her. We'll open Grandma Susie's gifts first, as we have done every Christmas, but hers will be the hardest, this year, to bear.

HEROIN CHRISTMAS

"I can't understand all the fuss about the birthday of one Jewish guy. Darn, hardly anyone celebrates mine," an old friend — a Holocaust survivor — says, when I call to conduct my rigorous post-mortem of the recent debacle.

What's it all about, anyway? "On its own merits Christmas would wither and shrivel in the fiery breath of universal hatred," wrote Bernard Shaw, in long-ago days, before the season's excesses were thrust upon us by shopkeepers and the press. In my books even Shaw waxed sentimental at Christmas.

GLUTTONY, ENVY, INSINCERITY, GREED. Enjoy Your Christmas. Two public-spirited grinches spent $1,200 — the amount they claim they would usually spend buying presents — on a billboard message at the side of the Trans Canada highway near Victoria that outraged many traditional Christians, delighted iconoclasts, but at least got a lot of people talking about what December 25th is meant to be. Now that the day itself has come and gone and the VISA bills are making holes in mail bags across the country, I prepared myself for the inevitable after-Christmas question, which comes on the heels of "All ready for Christmas?" and that is, "How did your Christmas go?" But this year there's been a change. The question I am asked most frequently at the bank, post office, pharmacy, liquor store — insincerely, but with infinite goodwill — is, "So . . . did you survive Christmas?"

Survive is something you do (if you're lucky) a holocaust, breast cancer, raising teenagers, a divorce. Christmas is supposed to be . . . what? A holly jolly deck the halls kind of ho ho ho whole family get together even though you don't speak to one another the other 364 days of the year.

My daughter's best friend shares a birthday with the Jewish guy we make all the fuss about, and on Christmas morning Charlotte called to wish her a Happy Birthday. Her friend's father answered the phone, full of overproof cheer. "This is Christmas day," he said, in case Charlotte came from another planet. "This is a very bad time."

"Where's his goddamn Christmas spirit!" Charlotte said when she put down the phone. "Something harsh must have happened to him when he was a kid. He should — get over it!".

It's not as if Christmas has always been peace on earth at our house, either. There was Heroin Christmas, where Mum threw a brick through Dad's truck window and Dad drove off anyway to spend Christmas holed up at the Super Eight Motel. There was PMS Christmas when Mum over imbibed and ran out into the road in her flaming red flannelette nightie, lay down on the white line and cried, "Hit me, nearest semi." (One car passed, the driver rolled down his window and shouted, what else? "Merry Christmas!") How will my daughters process these Christmases when they grow up? Will I call to wish my grandchildren compliments of the season and be told, "Mother, this is Christmas. It's a very bad time"?

What happened to the magic, the Christmases I knew as a kid? I still have warm memories of freezing in the woods while my father hacked down a tree, and getting the tree home in the trunk of the car without getting arrested by the RCMP (he didn't believe in permits).

And then there was the year my brother died. My mother had contracted German measles during her pregnancy and carried him, lifeless, inside her, through the holidays, without letting anyone know. "He had to come to term," she explained. When I asked why the baby wasn't induced, she wasn't certain why. "That's just the way it was back then. I felt like a walking coffin."

Maybe this is what Christmas is about: giving the impossible at a time when your heart could break. My mother baked shortbread, decorated the tree, stuffed the turkey, and opened each gift we'd made for her with the appropriate exclamation of glee. For us she must have squeezed out of herself every desperate last drop of joy to have it be, in that unimaginable time for her, Christmas as usual.

A sincere thank-you note, I have tried to impress upon my kids, will transcend all manner of social situations.

"Dude," my oldest wrote on a Post-It note she stuck on the bathroom mirror where her sister would be sure to see it. "Remember when I went out last night I asked you please not to eat those last two chocolates that Grandma sent me for Christmas? I was really looking forward to eating those chocolates, but when I got home they were gone so I guess you went ahead and ate them anyway. I hope you are sorry. Thanks a lot!!!"

Her sister replied with a Post-It of her own: "I am NOT sorry I ate your chocolates. They were YUMMY!!!"

This happened the day I had planned to lock them in a room with the Emotional Moments stationery they got in their stockings, to pen their Christmas thank-you letters.

"Thank-you note writing is one of the loveliest traditions to have been utterly compromised by the information age," writes Leslie Harpold, in *The Morning News*, an online magazine. Like many people, my daughters have grown used to firing off emails; they risk losing touch, I fear, with the concept of simple — but important — handwritten thank-you notes.

Harpold recommends a six-point formula. First greet the Giver, as in "Dear Uncle Richard." Then express your gratitude: "Thank you for the inflatable life-size moose. It is just what I always wanted."

My daughters complain I am asking them to be dishonest in thanking a seldom-seen relation for something they don't have time to blow up. Eventually I concede: they can drop the "what I always wanted" part if they at least write, "Thanks for the inflatable moose."

Discuss use of said gift, Harpold continues, and don't lie. "The moose is such a realistic shade of brown" is more honest than, "The moose makes our living room so much more cozy and warm."

In the next paragraph, mention the past . . . "It was great to see you at Grandma's funeral . . . " and allude to the future . . . "I look forward to seeing you again when Grandpa's time comes."

Next, repeat expression of gratitude. It's not overkill to say, "Thanks again for the moose!" though the person who sends a note in gold-ink embossing — "May the Lord Reward Your Kindness" — for the jar of dilled pickles (albeit homemade) perhaps got carried away.

Finally, the Regards (as in "Peace out, Shorty"). Do not include details of your life, i.e. complaints that your mother will gouge your eyes out with a fork if you don't finish this. The thank-you note is exclusively about thanking someone for their kindness, Harpold says. Simple as it sounds.

Simple, my kids say, sounds hard. So I stoop to bribery letting them in on the hidden, unspoken agenda behind thank-you notes: it will mean they are likely to be the recipients of further gifts. That isn't the best reason to write but, if your godfather sends you a "flat present" (the godfather's term for a fat cheque) and you don't acknowledge it, next Christmas he's going to think twice before sending you "a little something, it's really nothing." And, no, "Dude, thanks for the chump change, you rock" isn't going to make the godfather spontaneously cough up more, unless it's for a finishing school in the Alps.

My youngest, who is determined to practise law as soon as she hits legal age, argues I've given her the best reason not to write thank-you notes to those who regularly give her gifts she doesn't use. "If I write to Aunt Janet, thanking her for *another* crocheted toilet seat cover, it will encourage her," she says. She *would* have to bring up the crocheted toilet-seat cover. Five years ago I made the mistake of saying "One of these years Aunt Janet is going to surprise us and come up with a really original gift, like another crocheted toilet-seat cover."

By the end of the day I suggest we get started. "Just write the first word, 'Dear . . . ,'" I implore.

"How can I call someone "dear" when I haven't seen him since I was in utero?" my oldest daughter challenges.

I ignore her point and soldier on. "Express your gratitude. Do not begin with "I am just writing to say . . . " Clearly you don't need to say you are "just writing" because if Uncle Richard is sober enough to be reading your letter, it's obvious that you have written. Write as if what you say is happening now, in this very moment."

What is happening now, in this very moment, is that my daughters have left the table to smoke a doobie. My mother had a rule that we weren't allowed to play with our toys until we had finished our thank-you notes: "You will not smoke dope until you've written to your cousin thanking him for his generosity," I shout after them.

"The Herb Man say never put nothing in writing," my legal eaglet fires back. She's right; the last time he got acquitted he wore a T-shirt to court saying, "Nobody Talks, Everybody Walks". I scratch Cousin Herb off the list: we can thank him in person the next time we see him out of wiretape range.

When my daughters return to the bargaining table they want to know who else they "are allowed" to thank in person. "Like, what about Dad?"

For Christmas their father had made them a photograph album of his daily regime in the federal penitentiary.

"Here's the rule: if you live under the same roof, you don't have to write a thank-you note. Don't give me that *if Dad were here he wouldn't handcuff us to the chair* . . . why can't you just be thoughtful and write him a wretched thank-you note, for God's sake. You know how much mail means . . . you wouldn't even have been *born* if it weren't for him."

When all else fails, there's the guilt-inducing plea.

WHERE CHILDREN DECIDE
THEY DON'T WANT TO LIVE

I was at our home on the Queen Charlotte Islands when the call came from the hospital, and my twelve-hour trip back to Victoria became a long day's journey into the dark night of the soul. While other mothers sat snipping price tags off the latest back-to-school fashions, I sat by my daughter's bed in the Intensive Care Unit on the Pediatrics Ward watching her vital signs blip across a screen. She hadn't heeded the advice of the fine print on the bottle of Tylenol's label: "It is hazardous to exceed the maximum recommended dose . . . "

It could have been worse. A friend who'd stayed in our house the previous spring had left behind a tote bag containing what I assumed to be a writer's survival kit: a flask of Jameson's, a tube of smoker's toothpaste, a bottle of Acetaminophen with Codeine, and another unmarked vial of little orange pills. They looked a lot like children's aspirin, but since my friend suffers from indigestion, I took them to be his stomach medication. When he didn't call to ask if he had left his kit behind, remembering what I'd learned from my mother — never keep unlabelled drugs around because someone could eat them thinking they were aspirin — I threw the pills in the trash.

The day our daughter was released from hospital my friend — back in town — came to our house. When I finally remembered to ask him about the survival kit, he said he'd figured he must have left it behind in some lonely motel room on his drive back east. The orange pills were morphine — his editor's wife had died of cancer and bequeathed them to him in her will, lest he, too, one day wish to shortcut life's deteriorating processes. My friend's an old Boy Scout whose motto is "Be Prepared". He never leaves home without his passport (lest the urge to go somewhere suddenly overtake him), or enough drugs (should he fall terminally ill himself) to allow him to make one last, unambiguous, irrevocable decision — to take charge of his own destiny, like a captain going down with his ship.

There are desperate suicides and cunning suicides; people who do it to cause their loved ones pain and people who do it to save others the grief. There are deranged exhibitionists holding up traffic while they threaten to leap from bridges, and secretive souls who swim out into the ocean's anonymity. But the helplessness we feel when a child attempts or commits suicide is horrific beyond any stunt of self-annihilation an adult may indulge in. Edward Hoagland in his essay "The Urge for an End", wrote, "It would be hard to define chaos better than as a world where children decide they don't want to live."

My daughter learned the consequences of attempting to prematurely end her life. People took her seriously. "Committing" suicide (and even though courting the idea is different from engagement to the real impulse, it is a commitment) makes everyone uncomfortable because it appears to cast a subversive judgement upon our whole social order: that what was supposed to work in life — love, family, caring friends — did not. And furthermore, it "frightens the horses in the street" as Virginia Woolf once defined anti-social behaviour (before she walked into a river with a pocketful of rocks).

Distraught family and friends never stopped asking the question: why? *Was she depressed? Bored? Was she taking drugs?*

SUSAN MUSGRAVE

Was she abused as a child? Was she being bullied at school? They
struggled to find reasons. *It was a cry for help. She wanted
attention, sympathy from her peers. She needed therapy. She was
thirteen. They think they are immortal at that age.*

My daughter tried, for everyone else's sake, to come up
with an answer. "My best friend tried to kill herself that night
and I didn't want her to be alone." (She, too, lived.) "I missed
Dad." (He went to prison five years ago). "I missed Mum." (I
was out of town.) "I had a fight with my boyfriend." And the
clincher, when she was trying her hardest to wriggle out of an
appointment with the Kids at Risk counselor: "I wasn't trying
to kill myself. I did it for the rush. I wanted to get high."

The truth is, she had no clear idea why she emptied the
contents of our medicine cabinet into her stomach. But she
was adamant about one thing: she wouldn't try it again. Which
worried the counsellor. If she didn't know why she did it the
last time, how could she be so *sure* it wouldn't happen again?

I take comfort in what I have come to believe — that not
wanting to live was, for my daughter, "just a phase". When I
was her age I did the same thing: hacked my way into my veins,
choked down pills by the fistful, not understanding what it
meant to die, but not wanting to do less than live, either. I had
great expectations, matched only by great disappointments.
There was, I felt, a somber, imponderable fate.

Having survived far longer than I ever imagined I would
("Kill me if I make twenty-five," I told friends; I didn't believe
I'd have the capacity — mental or physical — to commit self-
murder after that doddery old age) I've learned to settle for
what comes my way — for the moment. I know the rush of
death comes soon enough for those of us patient enough to
live, and wait.

HELLO? MUMMA?

Bearing in mind the slogan, "If you love something, let it go free", I had put my sixteen-year-old daughter on a plane to spend a month in Australia with my goddaughter. I'd found a seat-sale ticket and got her a valid passport. I'd set her up with a bank card; every four days I would transfer fifty dollars into her account so she would have spending money. What must I have been thinking?

An email from my goddaughter's mother came two days later. "The Eagle has landed." I flew north where I planned to have a carefree teenager-free life at my home on Haida Gwaii.

Her phone card alone cost fifty dollars a day. My daughter, weeping over the long distance, said she'd been locked out of her lodgings by accident and was camping in a strip mall on Downer Street. The pay phone had a ring of lip gloss around it because she'd been talking to her friends on Vancouver Island all day. There was nothing else to do in Australia; she'd spent $200 on new sunglasses (I'd given her a VISA card with a $500 limit "for emergencies") but it hadn't stopped raining since she'd arrived. She'd seen no wildlife, except for some gross birds that tried to steal her last cigarette. She had only seen one good-looking boy and he was underage. All the kids she'd met were into crystal meth, and they wanted her to try it, too; would I buy her a ticket home, instead?

What was a mother to do? I'd loved her, let her go, and now she wanted to boomerang back. I tried not to panic, then went on the Internet, Googling "Things to do in Adelaide when you are 16". What I found wasn't hopeful:

"unless u wanna go to a museum or church there is hardly nething fun to do. me and my friend had an idea so ill share it wit u. it mite keep u amused for a day, or 5. depending on how good u can read bus timetables! what u do is just catch random busses around so u get totally lost. wen u get somewhere good pretend ur tourists, and hook up wit guys youll never c again! at the end of the exciting day . . . try to get home!"

I emailed my friends: did they have any ideas as to what might keep my daughter occupied in a less random way? "It would be great if my daughter could see more than the inside of a pay phone booth, though that in itself could be a rich experience," I wrote, trying to stay positive.

"Remember that song by Shell Silverstein, 'Hello mudda, hello fadda' about being at camp?" my friend, Lorna wrote, in response to my desperate email. "The chorus is 'Take me home, oh mudda, fadda, take me home,/ I hate Granada/ Don't leave me/out in the forest where/ I might get eaten by a bear.' Then a couple of stanzas, later, 'Waita minute,/It's stopped raining/guys are swimming/guys are sailing/playing baseball/gee, that's better/ mudda, fadda kindly disregard this letta.'"

I remembered the song, all right, but my recollection of summer camp was that it had *never* stopped raining and we were forced to stay indoors and participate in drug-induced Satanic rituals and underage orgies (of which I remember little since we were hypnotized first).

Another friend, Marilyn, replied, "Just about everybody I know who has sent a kid 'abroad' has a similar story. The only one that didn't work out was the one who helped her son come home early — a mistake, I think." A third, Marion, wrote that she had sent her daughter to Calgary for a respite when she was seventeen. "She spent most of her first days on the phone . . . fearing she was missing all that was happening in bad old Sidney." The consensus seemed to be that my daughter would fend for herself, find out something about the world, and, after a week or so, want me to disregard her initial homesickness.

My friends were right — The Eagle survived. She befriended a boy who collected trollies in the supermarket parking lot, and got to see the inside of an Australian parking lot as well as the phone booth at the mall. She photographed wildlife in a zoo. She witnessed a purse-snatching (by some crystal-meth addicted youths) and helped police retrieve the victim's purse. She partied with new friends who drove her to the airport to catch her plane back to Canada on her last day . . . which is when I got the final, most heart-rending phone call of all.

"Hello? Mumma? My passport's been stolen. They won't let me on the plane. Help me, mumma. I just want to come home!"

"In this world you must be a bit too kind in order to be kind enough"; wise words uttered by Pierre Marivaux, the French dramatist, way back in the seventeenth century. This begs the question: of what value is a kind heart in today's world?

In Buddhist practice we are asked to consider how to live well by reflecting on our death. Imagine yourself on your deathbed — tomorrow or next week or sometime over the next few years — then cast your memory back and bring to mind two good deeds you have done, two things that were kind.

If you are like me and can't recall anything to feel swell about in the good deed department, maybe you need to lower your standards. Almost everyone who is able to come up with acts of kindness they have unleashed upon the earth discovers them to be remarkably ordinary, not grandiose. "In life we cannot do great things," Mother Teresa said. "We can only do small things with great love."

For some people a true moment of goodness was simply the one where they told their father they loved him before he died. In our family, where feelings are never approached head-on, my brother, who sat by my father's side, was only able to blurt, "Susan loves you," partly because I wasn't there and mostly because he didn't want to embarrass my father by getting personal at the end.

For other people kindness can mean letting the person with one or two items behind them in line at the grocery store go ahead. "When someone is trying to merge into my lane in traffic, I always let him in," a friend says. "That is the only good deed I can come up with in my whole life."

Before speaking your mind, the Sufi's suggest, ask yourself this: is it true, is it necessary, is it kind? A dear and generous Irish relation once chastised me for speaking unkindly to my father (my upbringing had been a little Old Testament). Dick Musgrave's scolding left a deeper impression on me than being told I was selfish, or a disgrace to the family name, which, sadly, is what I remember of my father's hard words to me when I was growing up. On a trip to Ireland in 1976, my father must have goaded me about settling down and doing something productive with my life; "Just because you think *your* life has been a failure," I cried, "you don't need to take it out on me!"

Cousin Dick reproached me. "That was *very* unkind of you to say your father was a failure." He was right. What I had said may have been true, even necessary in the payback-time category, but it certainly wasn't kind. I can still burn with shame when I think of my father's hurt look, and since then I've tried my mightiest to be kind, or, at the very least, to *act* as if I were.

For instance, there was an incident in Bogota, Colombia, on a muggy afternoon: I was six months pregnant, sick, and had spent the day trying to find an envelope big enough to send a manuscript home to Toronto. I had finally hailed a taxi that wasn't occupied, and had opened the door when a crone, five times my age, half my height, wrapped in black from head to toe, elbowed me in the belly, ensconced herself in my seat, slammed the door, and locked it after her. Loving kindness, I reminded myself as I stood boiling on the curb with my can of Tear-Gas Paralyzer — to protect me from the unkindness of strangers, narco-terrorist kidnappers and the like — in hand. Tolerance. Unconditional love. My mood didn't last. By the time I'd slogged the three miles home in the humidity I told my husband what the old bat needed was an unconditional bullet in the head.

To my credit, at least I'd acted as if I were kind. I recall another day when I became, for a couple of hours, the embodiment of compassion — the day I met a distressed woman on my afternoon walk who asked me for a glass of water. I took her home where she confessed that she was an alcoholic coming down off a binge. She wanted me to call AA; the curmudgeon who came to counsel her said she was lucky I was a kind person who hadn't called the police. The police! She asked for water, not my money or my life.

Of what value is a kind heart in today's heart-breaking reality? There's only one answer: you can't be kind enough.

YOU'RE IN CANADA NOW, MOTHERFUCKER

The Political

SYMBOLISM UNDONE:
BREAKING OUT OF HANDCUFFS WITHOUT KEYS

September 30, 1995

"Don't hang up!" pleaded the editor who called to ask me for a writer's perspective on, what else but . . .

It's a sad fact. The splitting apart of our country is of so little interest that an editor has to beg a writer not to hang up at the very mention of "the referendum".

Don't stop reading! If you read on I promise you — among other things — a new approach to oral sex in western Canada.

I can hear the Reform party shaking its head. Must a writer stoop to oral sex in order to hook readers? Or is it just that we have become numb, Meeched-out, accord-less, too media-bludgeoned to have anything left to say about . . . tedium tedium . . . "The Neverendum"?

A Toronto poet I know sent a fax to Mike Harris yesterday saying now that the Conservatives are reducing the deficit by crushing the poor, he plans to move to Quebec and vote *OUI*. Indeed, as Andre Gagnon, the folksinger, suggested, maybe the rest of Canada should take a vote, separate, and *join* Quebec.

I suppose you'd find some opposition in the west, where our own separatist extremists add their vote to the YES side with bumper stickers saying GO QUEBEC GO, and the majority grump about having to read French on their

Cornflakes boxes. "I won't have French rammed down my throat" is the common cry, one more likely having to do with repressed Calvinist attitudes towards oral sex (it might lead to dancing) than bilingualism. (Well, I promised, didn't I?)

Parizeau, it is said, wants a divorce from Canada, while maintaining bedroom privileges. "Either way, it won't make any difference to the rest of us in this country," says a politician friend. Seriously, whether or not Quebecers vote *OUI* or *NON* on October 30th seems a remote reality to many in the west, and of less consequence than, say, whether or not DNA could have been planted on O.J.'s left sock. We have work, families, the everyday chaos of living well, putting one well-worn loafer in front of the other.

Take the first day of school. I drive to pick my daughter up from Grade One, French Immersion. I am delighted to glimpse her on the playground surrounded by new friends, until I take a closer look. One of them, a boy dressed in full RCMP regalia (it's two months until Halloween) is shouting at my daughter, "Speak English! Speak English!" and handcuffing her to his belt. She is singing — oblivious, it seems, to the politics that begin at home, or on the playground — as he leads her off the jail inside the jungle gym, *"Bonjour, mes amis, bonjour."*

When I have broken my daughter out and picked the lock on the cuffs, she hands me a scrap of paper with Corporal Tyler's phone numbers on it. "He has two numbers," my daughter says. "His parents split apart." Not separated, not divorced, but split apart. Instantly I feel sympathy for the little tyrant, and wish I hadn't been so rough on his handcuffs.

My politician friend thought every complex detail of this schoolyard scenario symbolic of what is going on in the rest of Canada. In the end, however, I don't think symbolism matters. Human beings matter, and politics, like symbolism, seems to get in the way of what is happening on the most obvious, commonplace levels, where we live our lives. Now I am one of the first to moan when I turn, always, to the French instructions on the cake mix box. Still, the image of my six-year-old being led off to the slammer because she wants to say "*Mon* Canada includes Quebec", in a small way — the way a wedge goes in at first — split me apart on the playground that day.

We are all being split, every day. Split along lines of gender, language, race. What upset me most, when O.J. Simpson was acquitted, was the number of African American males on TV punching the air with their clenched fists, as if victory were ever as black or white as guilt or innocence, *OUI* or *NON*.

Back in January I sat, along with a dozen other English and French Canadian writers, on a committee to rewrite the Oath of Canadian citizenship. The current oath is simply a long list of promises to be made to Queen Elizabeth the II, Her Heirs, Her Successors, Her Small Waddling Dogs, etc. It was unanimous: the Queen was to be axed. After her execution we split into two groups: the English writers remained to draft a new Canadian oath; the French writers went out on their own to write their version. The two new pledges were surprisingly similar, except for a solitary word — diversity. The English writers wanted new citizens to "respect all people, in their diversity." The French writers scrunched up their faces at this troublesome concept.

To us it meant we should accept people for their positive differences. The French writers said no: diversity meant "dividedness", and had negative connotations.

How quickly we became polarized. To break the ice, one writer asked the Minister when these new pledges might be introduced. Then John Gray piped up, "Is there any point in having an oath of Canadian citizenship when we don't even know if we are going to have one country?"

A terrible sadness fell over the room. One of the French writers said she could feel the pain coming from all of us, a physical weariness of spirit that seemed to suck all our words, our politics, our dreams, out of the room. We sat in silence, and then two people spoke at the same time, one in English, the other in broken English. Two small voices. "We didn't know you cared."

Bonjour, mes amis, bonjour.

THE CANADIAN SPECIFIC

I suspect it was from my father, who greatly admired New York because the traffic lights were synchronized (they weren't, he never stopped pointing out, in Victoria), and London, because they had "architecture", that I got the idea Canada was a provincial backwater colourlessly imitating the most soulless aspects of everything American or British. In 1964, when we acquired our own distinctive flag, my father insisted on flying the Jolly Roger on board our boat. He would never be caught flying "that nosebleed", as he dubbed the Maple Leaf.

My father was a third generation Vancouver Islander; when the BC Ferries began operating between Vancouver and the Island, he would sail across their bows, maintaining that steam gave way to sail. He believed nobody from the mainland had any business cluttering up our highways, either. As a boy he'd been one of the first to enroll at Shawnigan Lake School; as kids we were regaled with stories of how he had to crack the ice on winter mornings before taking a swim — and that was after fighting off the cougar. Somewhere along the way his roughing-it-in-the-bush lifestyle was interrupted and he was transplanted to an English boarding school — Berkhamstead — where his moment of glory was being caned by Graham Greene's father, headmaster there at the time. Perhaps he had all the love — for his homeland and anything smacking of homesickness — beaten out of him.

When I was at school in the 60s, a teacher assigned an essay to be entitled "My Nationality". Most of us, on gentile southern Vancouver Island, wrote, "English and Irish," or "Scottish on my mother's side." There was an occasional German grandmother or Swedish grandfather in the woodpile, but I can't recall a single one of my classmates saying, "I'm a Canadian."

I grew up knowing little about my own country. When I began writing I set all my stories elsewhere — in New York, London, and Rome — believing that nothing of any importance had ever happened on my own little postage stamp of soil. I was led to believe I had inherited my creative writing genes from the "Irish" side of the family, though it became clear to me that all writers we learned about at school were either dead or lived in England. Which was where I decided to go (having read Sylvia Plath, I knew that death was not only inevitable but importantly imminent) if I lived long enough to apply for my own Canadian passport.

I did live to see eighteen, and to get a passport. When I travelled to England and further afield to the continent, in the early 70s, I was in for a surprise. Wherever I went I found Canadians of all nationalities, especially Americans, wearing the Maple Leaf stitched to their rucksacks or pinned conspicuously to their lapels. Being Canadian, I learned, meant you were neutral, but in a good, clean, friendly, wide-open-spaces sort of way. Whatever we were, it seemed many of the young travellers I met wanted to be us.

Leaving my country had the effect of turning me into one of the greatest lovers this country has ever had. One of the greatest lovers of this country. What I am trying to say is, absence made the heart grow patriotic. I love my country. Even though we have been labelled the vichyssoise of nations —

cold, half French and difficult to stir — we are honestly everything we pretend to be: one nation of eighty ethnic groups who still base our fashion taste on what doesn't itch.

As Canadians we have always used up a lot of skull space figuring out who we are. "Canadians are unarmed Americans with health care," a comic quipped on TV. It's true; you won't find ARMED RESPONSE on any Rosedale lawns, or bumper stickers threatening "Insured by Smith and Wesson", but I did see a Post-It note in the rear window of a car parked on Hastings Street in Vancouver: ATTENTION PLEASE ETHICALLY DISORIENTED INDIVIDUALS AND PERSONS WITH A PHARMACOLOGICAL PREFERENCE, THERE IS NOTHING WORTH STEALING INSIDE THIS VEHICLE. SORRY FOR THE INCONVENIENCE. HAVE A NICE DAY.

What else, besides unarmed but covered, are we? A polite, well-mannered lot: Americans say no to drugs; Canadians say no thank you. The average Canadian says "I'm sorry" 4.3 times a minute. Even if you bump into a fellow Canadian causing him to spill his latte on his lumberjack shirt, chances are he will mutter "I'm sorry" before you get a chance to sputter it yourself.

Pierre Berton defined a Canadian as someone who knows how to make love in a canoe. "A Canadian is someone who drinks Brazilian coffee from an English teacup, and munches a French pastry while sitting on his Danish furniture, having just come from an Italian movie in his German car. He picks up his Japanese pen and writes to his Member of Parliament to complain about the American takeover of the Canadian publishing business," wrote Campbell Hughes back in 1973. Eugene Whalen, Agricultural Minister under Pierre Trudeau, said some Canadians are so dumb they keep their tomatoes in the fridge (refrigeration causes tomatoes to lose their flavour:

I didn't know, either). As for Trudeau himself, the poet Irving Layton paid him a (typically Canadian) backhanded compliment: "In Pierre Elliot Trudeau Canada has at last produced a political leader worthy of assassination."

"Canada is so square even its female impersonators are women," claimed a character in the 1983 film, *Outrageous*. We may be square, but we are fair and square, a just people, who believe everyone should have their share, and that all things come to those who wait — usually in a lineup. Back in the days when we used to hold Beauty Contests, the writer Andreas Schroeder said that in Canada we would award the prize to the runner-up on the grounds that the girl who should have won already had enough going for her.

"Hockey is the Canadian specific," wrote the poet Al Purdy who described the game as a cross between murder and ballet. There has been only one authenticated attack by a wolf on a man in Canada, and that man was not Farley Mowatt. The average Canadian uses ten pounds of salt a year — and that doesn't include what he puts under his tires. The majority of Canadians consider life too short to stuff a mushroom and think poutine is French cuisine. It took 142 years and seventeen treaties to finalize the American-Canadian border. Canadians raise over four billion worms a year for export. In some parts of the country ten bowling shirts are still considered a great wardrobe.

One sure sign of a country that feels comfortable outside its own borders is its ability to laugh at itself. We can laugh, for example, at our generally law-abiding, good-natured national temperament.

Q: "How do you get twenty-five drunken Canadians out of your swimming pool?"

A: "You say, 'Excuse me, please, would you all mind leaving?'"

~ ~ ~

It wasn't just my travels abroad that broadened my Canadian horizons; it was discovering Canadian writers, also. Two poets in particular: Irving Layton, who wrote about sex, I discovered while sitting out a detention in the school library, and Earle Birney, who wrote about death. Birney was the first non-English, non-dead poet we studied at school and he wrote about his last day on a mountain when he had to decide whether or not to push his unlucky friend, who has already fallen halfway off a cliff, all the way over. A very Canadian situation. It was left to the class to decide: did he or didn't he? And if he did, did he say "sorry" afterwards?

My father long ago moved on to that country where all flags fly at half-staff, in perpetuity. I'm sorry to say he would turn apoplectic in his grave if he could see me now, dusting off the patio furniture for a Canada Day salmon barbecue on Sunday — the Maple Leaf forever wired to my Mazda's antenna.

EN ROUTE

I am not a terrorist. The only bombs I carry in my luggage these days are bath bombs. The button I wear on my lapel — a souvenir from my last peace march in 1969 — says BAN THE BOMB, which does not mean I intend to commandeer Air Canada Jazz and slam into the Parliament Buildings to protest the re-election of the Liberals in British Columbia. I am with Jesus on this one: when he said love your enemies, he didn't mean kill them.

My mother is afraid that if I make jokes about Airport Security they will ban me from flying. These days you can't easily sneak through under an alias, either; every time you pass a person in uniform they demand to see photo identification.

Ever eavesdropped on the conversations these people who scan your hand luggage for cuticle scissors and computers (surely even a terrorist would know a laptop's the first place they check for explosives these days) are having? In the past months I've overheard one debate on the laxative properties of bran muffins, the details of a Friday night date that bombed, and the sad plight of a mother-in-law who is going to a home if she doesn't start being nicer to the family mutt. At the Vancouver airport I heard a pilot pleading to be allowed to keep his dead grandmother's nail clippers. Let him have them, I thought. Who wants an overwrought pilot who can't work the controls because his fingernails need trimming?

Why sweat the minutiae, making us forfeit so many of our rights and toiletries going through Security, when today's hijacker thinks nothing of packing a time-bomb in amongst his clean underwear, and blowing himself, and everyone else on the plane, to kingdom come?

You don't even have to be a terrorist when it comes to dreaming up new ways to murder your fellow passengers. Shoelaces can be used to strangle the guy who tries to commandeer your armrest. The razor blade inside your pencil sharpener could slit the throat of the kick-boxing enthusiast for whom in-flight entertainment means pummelling the back of your seat for the flight's duration. I figure if they want to make sure we behave, Security should require all passengers to wear straightjackets on board commercial flights; frills like going to the bathroom should be nixed, too, in the name of Zero Tolerance.

Meanwhile, Airport Security must be accumulating a mighty collection of seized artifacts to auction off on eBay. Perhaps they could make a donation to our struggling national airline who could then offer their passengers something more substantial than pretzels and tank water.

In case you're like me and didn't know it, Air Canada no longer serves food on flights less than three hours and twenty minutes in duration. The taste of the water (which, I was assured, was "potable") to wash down the pretzels I was issued on another recent flight brought back painful memories of the holiday I spent visiting many of Mazatlan's picturesque public conveniences.

When I inquired as to whether Air Canada had acquired a bulk rate deal on surplus water from Walkerton, Ontario, a travel-weary flight attendant told me they had no space on board to store bottled water. She offered to "smuggle" me some Evian water from Business Class. Evian, of course, is "naive" spelled backwards, but at least you can't see the impurities.

No room on a 767 for fresh drinking water? What has become of all the space where the meal trays were once stowed? Perhaps it has been converted into an in-flight morgue for the bodies of passengers who die from dehydration.

Here's an idea. Air Canada could take up the slack from Corrections Canada: no more steak and lobster dinners "on demand" for prisoners in federal penitentiaries. Instead, first time offenders could do hard time on board flights (with get-tough-on-crime names such as Air Canada Slam or Air Hokey-Pokey) from Vancouver to St. John's, with nothing but pretzels and tank water, for the duration of their sentences. Those who object can bail, at no further expense to the taxpayer. I guarantee we'd have no repeat offenders.

All joking aside, Airport Security is the only place I've ever done time where making a joke is a criminal offense. You can go directly to jail just for joking. Ask to call a lawyer — they think that's a joke, too.

But Airport Security has got to be the biggest joke. False-Sense-of-Security is more like it. As far as I know, none of the terrorists cracked side splitters as they slipped through Security on September 11th. Those folks (as Dubya dubbed them) were deadly serious. Wouldn't it make more sense to detain passengers who *don't* go through Security joking? Having a sense of humour should be a prerequisite for anyone boarding an airplane these days.

"Well, I learned a lot. You'd be surprised. They're all individual countries." Thus quoth Ronald Reagan, former U.S. president, following his 1982 tour of South America. If Ronnie had travelled north instead of south from Coca Cola-land, I fear he would not have reached the same profound conclusion. Even though we are one country made up of eighty ethnic groups living in eleven individual provinces, on the surface we don't seem a whole lot different from our armed American cousins who don't have health care.

From the end of the government dock in my home town on Vancouver Island, you can see Mt. Baker, snowcapped all year round, lording it over us like a dominatrix from the Washington State mainland. This mountain is so much a part of us that we have a saying in Sidney: "If you can see Mt. Baker today, it'll rain tomorrow. If you can't see Mt. Baker, it's raining now."

Mt. Baker gets photographed daily by visitors who stop to have a latte at Starbucks or a bite at the ubiquitous McDonald's. Our scenery, like our coffeehouses and drive-through restaurants, is American. My twelve-year old daughter even thinks *God* is American, religion being one more product we're sold on a daily basis — like Hollywood, like the War on Drugs.

I grew up gazing south across the straits to the Olympic Peninsula and American mountains that rose out of the sea into heaven. Even the scenery I learned about in school had the American flag waving over it — our highest peaks and largest lakes commemorate dead American presidents — like Mt. Eisenhower, Kennedy Lake. I thought God must have drawn a line along the 49th parallel, where the mosquitoes started biting, and called everything north of that line Canada. The long, undefended Canada-US border is perhaps all that delineates our differences.

I only became aware of our separateness from the States because my parents were smugglers. Nothing that would have landed them lead roles on *America's Most Wanted*, but, from my child's-eye-view, risky enough.

Every summer we sailed down to the San Juan Islands — the American equivalent of our Gulf Islands — where Americans post signs saying TRESPASSERS WILL BE SHOT to keep you from picnicking on their beaches. In Roach Harbour we were made to stay on board the boat while my father went ashore and cleared customs. Once we were legal aliens we were treated to American ice-cream cones while my father stocked up on his annual supply of Camels, which he hid in a rope locker under my bunk. My mother always invited Mr. Smith, the Customs and Immigration Officer in Sidney where we re-entered Canada, for a cup of tea, sitting him down on top of the contraband cigarettes. Every summer I worried that my Daddy would go to prison for his crimes, and that my mother would spend her days smuggling cigarettes into jail the way (I then believed) other visitors smuggled files in cakes.

My dad was a hard act for any man to follow, but eventually I found one — a smuggler from Washington State. Unlike my father, my future husband did not clear customs at the Canadian border, or serve tea when his freighter, loaded to the

SUSAN MUSGRAVE

gunwales with thirty tonnes of Colombian marijuana, broke down off the west coast of Vancouver Island. He brought it in to an inlet north of Tofino to make repairs and offloaded his cargo in the middle of the night. (These days importing pot would be like transporting coals to Newcastle, but in 1980 our province's main export was not BC Bud.) At daybreak the combined forces of the DEA, FBI, RCMP and Coast Guard descended — the ship had been under surveillance since leaving Barranquilla. The Colombian crew surrendered but one of the Americans took off up the beach, pursued by a Mountie and a tracking dog. The dog pinned the suspect under a log, taking formidable bites out of his desire to remain silent. "I give up!" the man cried. "I'm an American citizen! Don't I have any rights?"

The Mountie raised his rifle and brought the butt down on the smuggler's head. "You're in Canada now, motherfucker," he said.

Big mistake. By Canadian rights the Mountie should have asked the surrendered man whether he wished to be beaten in French or in English.

I don't know anyone who doesn't have their own cross-border smuggling story. I've smuggled emeralds from Colombia in my bra (they turned out to be worthless), panties from Victoria's Secret in Bellingham (they disappeared in the wash) socks from Socks du Jour in Seattle (my daughter purloined them). Luckily, I have nothing to show, i.e. no criminal record, for my efforts. Nothing, that is, but the red teapot I bought in Los Angeles in 1981. It cost me twenty-four dollars US and I have never declared it. Until now. I hope there's a statute of limitations but if there isn't, well, it'll be one load off my conscience as I sit in my prison cell sipping Iron Goddess of Mercy tea from a styrofoam cup.

The border has always been open, as far as I can see; most of us treat it like a kind of Honour System that encourages dishonesty. We drive to Blaine, an hour south of Vancouver, discard our kids' old clothes in duty-free shop washrooms, and drive back over the border to the True North strong and free, the kids dressed in multiple layers of back to school duty-free clothes. It's just so much easier to say "nothing to declare" than spend the day having your car taken apart wingnut by bolt because you declare the medicinal marijuana you carry with you for depression — which always hits after you take the kids shopping.

But face it, we're small beer. The big spenders don't pull into Customs and Immigration hauling guns or cocaine — they go around it. They use air space or the high seas — or leave their loot in some bushes at Roach Harbour (I wonder how it got its name?), ride the ferry home, clear customs, and return under cover of darkness, by cigarette boat, for their contraband.

Nothing to declare. It sounds hopeful, a Canadian prayer. Perhaps our national motto should be amended to read, "From sea to shining sea: Nothing to declare."

WILD SALMON DON'T DO OXYTETRACYCLINE

Cedar and salmon were our lifeblood once. Now, in British Columbia, we have a wilderness of stumps, and sea-pens full of diseased carnivores on drugs.

Once the salmon was monarch of the sea, a creature whose life cycle, a perfect circle, we studied in school. We watched scratchy filmstrips of the salmon being born in pure mountain streams, narrated with deep male authority. We followed the salmon as it swam out to sea where it performed a vital function, eating the slower swimmers. Then some Higher Fish Power guided the salmon back to the very place where it had begun; it spawned (this was where we started paying attention, though fish-sex looked as lonely to me as when humans attempted it) and died. Before the ravens chowed down on its eyes, a thousand tiny offspring were shooting back down to the sea.

These days the circle of life begins when a guy in gumboots mixes a whack of milt and a whack of roe in a five-gallon Chevron bucket, according to Andrew Struthers, a Vancouver Island writer who did time in a Tofino fish plant. The minute they are deemed tough enough to survive the saltchuk, the smolt are dosed with oxytetracycline and herded into giant open-mesh net cages suspended from anchored metal-cage frames.

Now these sea-pens full of fledglings have to be protected from predators. Fish farmers admit to shooting thousands of seals and sea lions each year because they rip the pen walls apart, hoping for a free lunch. Hundreds of crows — seagulls, too — get dispatched for trying to hone in on the feed the fish get seeded to them from a sack labelled NOT FOR HUMAN CONSUMPTION. In 1995, about 10.5 tonnes of feed medicated with antibiotics designed for humans — which, experts say, could lead to more antibiotic-resistant superbugs in the future — was produced for BC fish farms.

Why, then, is this fishy food full of antibiotics suitable for humans labelled NOT FOR HUMAN CONSUMPTION? It could have to do with the fact the feed has to be laced with orange pigment, there being no krill in captivity, which is what wild salmon eat and what makes them deliciously orange. Struthers says there are two kinds of pigment on the market. One is considered safe in America but toxic in Japan, the other okay-dokay in Japan but deadly in America. They have one thing in common, however. They are both orange.

And then there are the drugs. When a wild salmon gets stressed, and believe me they do, with all the lawsuits being waged over them (BC accusing Ottawa of treason; Ottawa suing BC for cancelling the US lease at Nanoose Bay to crank up fish talks; BC countersuing Ottawa; BC suing the US for stealing our fish) it often gets a kidney disease, and goes belly-up. The kidneys of feedlot fish, packed at ten kilograms per cubic metre in their underwater Auschwitzes (imagine you in your bathtub with two ten-pound Sockeyes leaping over you — that's how crowded it gets) are chopped liver, so to speak. That's why they get doped to the gills with (and we have a rule around our house: never eat anything you can't pronounce) Trimethoprim-sulfadiazine, Ormethoprim-sulfadimethoxine, Enrofloxacin, Erythomycin, Florfenicol, and of course more Oxytetracycline (which also means sewage into pristine BC coves equal to a city of 500,000 each day) so they'll live. At least until the farmer decides it's time for them to die, and cuts off their food supply to trim them up for harvesting. Struthers, in his book *The Green Shadow*, a must for anyone with an interest in wacko BC environmental politics, claims that after two weeks of starvation it's a fish-eat-fish world — or pencil stubs, beer caps, folded up tally sheets, all of which he has found inside the bellies of the beasts he has gutted, cleaned, scrubbed, and shipped to Vancouver to be eaten in upscale restaurants.

These days I'm saying NO THANK YOU TO DRUGS, and grilling my wild salmon on the gas barbecue again tonight. You know what they say about British Columbia: Super. Natural. While supplies last.

BETTER SAFETY THAN SORROW

"My choice of a life of adventure may well have been a result of the fact that action raised my blood pressure giving me enough energy to live," wrote the Polish writer, Jerzy Kosinkski. For him, life had to be a daring adventure — or nothing.

In our culture, these days, there is no core, no authenticity to our lives; we have become dangerously preoccupied with safety, have dedicated ourselves to ease. We live without risk, hence without adventure, without discovery of ourselves or others. The moral measure of man is: for what will he risk all, risk his life?

I like to think I'm a woman who takes risks. For starters, I get out of bed every morning, which, if you believe *Ripley's Believe It or Not*, is one of the biggest risks a person can take. Beds caused 77,581 injuries last year, aside from the fact that most people, after all, die in bed.

After eating a breakfast of Natural Life cereal and listening to the CBC tell me the greatest risk of cancer is from natural elements in food itself, I get ready to drive my daughter up the hill to catch her school bus. (When I was a kid I would have walked, but that was before pedophiles on day parole hung out behind every day-care centre.) Driving on the highway is by far the biggest risk. One in four Canadians has been injured in a car accident. Mondays and Tuesdays are the safest days on the road, but if you're driving on Saturday it's more important to wear clean underwear.

Every morning, at 7 AM we pass another mother, who lives closer to the school, escorting her daughter up the hill. The mother wears a vest with reflective yellow tape X'ed across her back. Some mornings I have to grip the wheel, as something older than the present organization of my civilized self takes hold of me. Do other mothers have murderous thoughts like this in the mornings? What makes me want to give the wheel a sharp left, and, for no apparent reason, run her down?

It's the oh-so-safety issue again, rearing its reflective head. An X-rated jacket, a plastic flag fluttering over the seat of a bicycle, and, yes, even those BABY ON BOARD stickers in the windows of boomer's vans, make me see red (a baby's life is worth slowing at a red light for, of course, but so is my eighteen-year-old daughter's and my seventy-five-year-old mother's). What these attention-getting devices say to me is, "*I* am here. *You* watch out." Why aren't people watching out for themselves? Or, better still, watching out for closet psychopaths like *me*?

They would no doubt say they *are*, which is why they are dressed like traffic cops or airport commissioners: they want to help *me* notice *them*. And they are right to be vigilant, of course — dead right. But while I am a person of immense compassion — I brake for small hapless children who fling themselves into the road trying to bite my tires, mother ducks jaywalking with their brood to the beach, dogs, cats, road kill, anything that slithers, jerks, or otherwise oozes life — adult pedestrians and people who want to save on gas should take responsibility for themselves.

Now that I've made my position clear and alienated three quarters of the population, my brother — who cycles to his government job every day — included, I'm hitting my stride. The thing is, life is *not* safe, no matter how much we try to legislate it to be. Kill Your Speed. Buckle Your Seat Belt. Fasten Your Crash Helmet. If You Drink Don't Drive. Say No to Drugs. I'm weary of people telling me how to live, what to eat, drink, inhale, or wear on a black night when I'm walking my pit bull. "Set the foot down with distrust on the crust of the world — it is thin," wrote the poet Edna St. Vincent Millay. No matter how thick the helmet covering the crust of your skull, you can still get tossed off that two wheeler into your next life. No matter how many layers of Kevlar your bambino wears to school, the yellow bus can still hit an icy turn, hurtling him into the sweet hereafter. I see babies dressed to the nines in Flame Retardant Material only, toddlers in the park wearing crash helmets on the swings. A kid can't jump on a trampoline without a spotter, play in the woods without a bodyguard, bicycle to the corner store for an ice-cream cone without a parent, and a personal taster, in tow. Life jackets in a canoe in the mid-Atlantic I'll go along with — caution no doubt has its place — but under the garden sprinkler or in the wading pool? *Loosen up, folks.* Each one of us is skating over a thin crust of ice on this earth, and our safety is in our speed.

Face it, life is dangerous. And then you die. You get buried with REST IN PEACE or SAFE AT LAST on your headstone. I say, over my dead body.

I aim to live, to postpone death by living life full throttle. By suffering, by loving, by making mistakes, by learning from my errors. By picking myself up, brushing myself off, and trying again. By *risking*.

"Do I sense a risk taker?" a psychiatrist I saw recently intoned. I was tired; I had Attention Deficit Disorder and Chronic Fatigue Syndrome that day and wanted drugs — all the prescription drugs he could give me to make the fast life go by even faster. He looked at me as if I had told him I wished to inject heroin with a turkey baster.

"A risk taker? Why wouldn't I be?" Then I quoted a Chinese proverb: *Of all the thirty-six alternatives, running away is best.* The psychiatrist recommended I spend the rest of my life in therapy. I got the impression he felt it was going to be a very short life.

She that leaves nothing to chance will do few things ill, but she will do very few things, I've told myself, all my life, from Day One when I back-pedalled away from kindergarten on a stolen tricycle. Too many rules for me in the Funhouse. Too many *thou shalt nots.* Nobody ever suggested *Thou shalt think for yourself.* No one ever told me, you have the *ability and the intelligence to learn things for yourself.*

~ ~ ~

"He is a thrill seeker, that guy," a woman trying to analyze my husband, came up with. "I asked why he never took up sky-diving and he said with a withering look, 'because you have to take a six-week course on how to prepare your fucking pack.'"

I don't think it's thrill-seeking so much as life-seeking. My husband, like most people, is no one thing. He may be a (thrill) seeker but he can also spend five nights sleeping with one-eye open on a cot beside our daughter in an understaffed hospital room where the underpaid nurses work to keep our children breathing. And he can sit through endless baseball games while she strikes out. Not way-killer thrilling at all, by my standards. But thrilling enough if you're that kind of dad.

Last summer a friend stopped by to take my daughter and me kayaking. By the time he had the emergency flares, the flotation devices, lifesaving equipment, ship to shore radios, waterproof matches, killer whale repellents, the fluorescent wet suits with Xs on the backs — all of it explained, itemized and repacked — I just wanted to go home and curl up with a good murder mystery. Why can't you just jump in a boat and push off anymore? Why must you be a graduate of an Emergency Response Team, have your Air Sea and Rescue certificate with a degree in celestial navigation before casting yourself adrift?

When we were kids, we just shed our clothes, slapped on Baby Oil, built a raft, lit a fire on board to cook our hot dogs, and paddled out over our heads into the sea. One time the fire burned through our raft and we all had to abandon ship; not one of us, it goes without saying, knew how to swim. We stayed in that icy water clinging to the wreckage until someone's father putted out to rescue us. Nowadays we'd be suing that father for wrecking our fun, and hence our child-hoods, the logging companies for creating driftwood, our parents for neglect, and the Parks Branch for not posting a notice, warning us not to light fires on board our wooden rafts to cook wieners.

It's our culture I am fed-up with, not the decent citizens of this country who are baffled and misled by everything from media to the lowest forms of government on down. We are subject to fifty-two million laws. My aim is to try and break one of them every day (small, innocuous ones, like entering at the EXIT sign) without getting caught. I'm not the type who would benefit from incarceration. If it isn't perfectly clear, I don't like anyone telling me what to do. I certainly don't want anyone else owning the keys to my front door.

So I'll have to behave. I promise not to run over any good people who are just trying to help drivers like me who may have less on their minds than watching out for pedestrians or cyclists. My brother says he has to wear a vest with a reflective X otherwise motorists don't give him a wide enough berth. His aim is to get to work every day without leaving his two young children fatherless.

The problem is — you're dead if you do, dead if you don't. We're so used to seeing pedestrians and cyclists decked out in the latest reflective *come hit me* gear that those who leave home without it are, as we used to say, accidents looking for a place to happen. Nowadays you're a victim, or you're vulnerable. Just look at the cougar in Port Alice who mistook an innocent cyclist for something to run down and entertain for dinner — nothing like a moving target to get those predatory juices flowing. Ain't no X going to save you, if nature — and sometimes even human nature — gets in the way.

This morning the reflective mum said goodbye to her daughter at the crosswalk. Her daughter did not look both ways before stepping out — or, if she did, I didn't see her. Her coat and jeans were the same black-blue colour as the rain slick road. She blended darkly with the light from the street lamp as it bounced back at me off the road, blinding my eyes.

I hit the brakes, veered to the left, skidded to a stop.

I just missed her. She didn't even see me.

She kept on walking as if her life depended on it.

THE THING THAT STRANGERS TAKE AWAY

November 11, 2001

"Where do all our memories go?" was the question my great-grandfather, mortally wounded in the First World War, most often asked my great-aunt during his last days. Towards the end he underwent surgery, and came out of the anaesthetic long enough to utter his final words: *sunt lacrimae rerum*. All things are weeping. Tears are the lot of the world.

What happens when, as we approach the end of our life, our memory begins to fail? Ralph Waldo Emerson, while attending the poet Longfellow's funeral, turned to a fellow mourner and said, "That gentleman had a sweet beautiful soul, but I have entirely forgotten his name."

Emerson resisted the loss of his memory by sticking labels onto everything, describing its function. Most touching was the name he pinned to his umbrella: "the thing that strangers take away."

Without memory we would not be able to ask ourselves the question most of us ask every time we open a newspaper or watch *Newsworld* on TV: to be or not to be, and for how much longer? We remember what we have survived, which gives us hope for the future. Memory is a way of making peace with time.

What could be more dangerous to civilization than those who *lack* memories? Those who forget because they must?

Those who live without hope? We make them into strangers, the people we fear: how can we understand those who willingly forfeit their own lives in order to take away ours?

To them, we are less than perfect strangers.

At a recent dinner party I talked with friends about our memories of war, those that have taken place in our own lifetime. Barbara, an American, remembered being taught to "duck and cover" beneath her desk, should an atom bomb drop on her school. Carole, born in London during World War II, remembers sleeping on a mattress under a war-issue cast-iron dining room table meant to protect her from falling debris, in the event of an air raid. Judith, who was a teenager in that war, remembers her brother going off to fight and feeling resentful (and guilty for feeling resentful) that *he*, like the brothers of all her girlfriends, was the centre of attention. She remembers blackouts and talk of a bomb being dropped on Estevan Point, on Vancouver Island, but not going off. I recall Mrs. Guest, my Grade Two teacher, who had been a prisoner of war in Japan, and the vaccination mark the size of a Mandarin orange on her arm, because, she told us, they used the same needle to vaccinate everyone. Joy, a second generation Japanese-Canadian, recalls being ousted from her home in Delta, B.C. to an internment camp in the Kootenies.

Most of us remember having to memorize "In Flanders Fields", (those were the days when "memory work" was mandatory; I recall, too, having to memorize poetry for school detentions) but the experiences of war and death were foreign to me, things that could only happen in another country. Full of youth and high ideals, I thought John McCrae's poem was not relevant to my world. I was too busy going on peace marches and burning my training bra to remember all those who had willingly forfeited their lives so that I might still have the freedom to disagree.

"Take up our quarrel with our foe . . . " I have forgotten much of that poem, but the images remain: rows of white crosses and, as another writer, Thomas Browne, put it, how "the iniquity of oblivion blindly scattereth her poppy".

It would be hard not to remember the images from September 11th, though some will forget because they must. For most it will be remembered as the day the world, as we have been lucky enough to have known it, changed. Tears may be our lot; is there much left to do but change our style of weeping?

My own memory has not deteriorated to the point where I have to attach a Post-It on my computer to remember its role, but if I want to remember something, I write it down. And, lest I forget where I've put that-which-I-must-not-forget, I back up my notes in my computer's memory bank.

If God has not completely forgotten us, he might reach out and attach a Post-It to our sorrowing planet: "the thing that strangers took away."

THE MINDLESS TOUCH

"Have you noticed that the war is over and something called the Olympics is on?" my daughter writes, in her weekly letter home. For the last fortnight, she says she has turned on the television, desperately seeking news, only to find all the channels preoccupied by figure skaters having a cry over gold medals while people are presumably still blowing each other up in Afghanistan. "But what's a war compared to coming first in ice skating?" she asks.

It's a bloodthirsty struggle to win — whether it be a war or the Olympics. Both, while promoting a great surge of national flag-flying pride, involve disinformation and deals made on the sly; both get big ratings, though the polls say the hockey game last Sunday attracted more viewers than bin Laden looking tired outside a cave. Both are worlds filled with weeping: with joy (on winning gold), with disappointment (on losing gold), or with grief when your loved one comes home in the same box as his medal for valour.

Perhaps these kinds of events that take place on the world stage have a more sinister purpose: to keep us preoccupied with what is going on *without* us so we don't have the inclination to search *within*. Being constantly distracted is, in itself, a form of searching: in our case it isn't the searching that's so much at fault; it's where we look.

Mention the word *gold* and we all become — like those mystics who stare, eyes wide open at the sun, seeking enlightenment — blind. Remember Nike's infamous billboard at the 1996 Atlanta games: You Don't Win Silver, You Lose Gold — the slogan that made that corporation a major loser in the eyes of a few diehards who still believe competitive sports are about *playing the game*. Life, inevitably, imitates ads, and the latest plague of gold-rush fever that began in Salt Lake City last month soon infected the world.

"Gold is a Girl's Best Friend" read the slogan-of-the-week at a gas station in my neighbourhood (last week's was "Most people know how to make a living but not how to make a life"). I have nothing against gold, per se — it's just that I've always found silver more understated and tasteful. I am against what gold stands for — the idea that you can't win anything less. You're only a winner if everything you touch turns to gold.

Understated, of course, is not what competitive sports or war is about, and whether or not gold can be called tasteful depends on the price. I think of my neighbours — their oldest son on the Olympic swim team shot himself in the basement the year his team didn't come first. Their middle son, same scenario; only he hanged himself four years later in the same basement. The remaining son, last I heard, was training to follow in his brothers' wakes.

Perhaps I have my parents to thank, for not pushing me hard enough to become competitive. Had I arrived home from the Olympics with a gold medal around my neck my mother would have thanked God that their good money hadn't been wasted on skating lessons. My father, who maintained that any fool can win, as long as there isn't a second entry, would have said, "let's see if you can do even better next year." They taught me a lesson I am still grateful for: I couldn't win.

The real winner in my mind is the one who stands in the middle of the ice and declares to the crowd, "I am going to fall," and laughs about it when she does. Or the Borstal boy in the film *The Loneliness of the Long Distance Runner*, who stops running just as he is about to win the race, and strolls towards the finish line while the competition streaks past. He knows he can win, that everybody expects him to win — they are even *betting* on him to win, in fact, — that winning is his get-out-of-jail-free card. He also knows that winning is beside the point.

I watched the film in the west of Ireland, years ago, with neighbours who had never travelled further than the pub at the end of the road. "Run, you fool," they cried, when the Borstal boy stopped. "Why does he stop? Go on, keep running, boy, run for your life."

The crowd looked at me as if I, being from a different culture, could make sense of it for them: why had he stopped?

I couldn't explain. When we all quit going for the gold, stop killing ourselves to win — might we not have a chance of attaining some sort of balance in our lives?

STILL WAITING FOR THE BARBARIANS

In "Waiting for the Barbarians", written in 1904, the Greek poet Cavafy describes the excitement building in the Roman forum where all have assembled — because the barbarians are due to arrive that day. Nothing is going on in the senate; no point in making laws, the senators say, because when the barbarians come *they* will do the legislating. The emperor at the city's main gate waits to receive their leader. The consuls and praetors are bedecked in gold and jewels because "things like that dazzle the barbarians." Decadence prevails. The distinguished orators don't bother to show up because the barbarians are coming today and they're bored by rhetoric and speeches.

And then — disappointment. The streets empty, the people, lost in thought, bewildered, and serious-faced, go home. Because it is nightfall and still the barbarians have not come. Word came from the north that there are no more barbarians.

"Now what's going to happen to us without barbarians?" Cavafy writes. "They were, these people, a kind of solution."

Life, since September 11th, 2001, has been somewhat anticlimactic. I keep waiting for the terrorists to do something, as the FBI keep promising they're going to do . . . any day now. If we just stay tuned to CNN. Something has to happen. So far it just seems like . . . more broken promises.

Maybe this is the terrorist's ultimate weapon: *nothing* is going to happen. They have done their best and their worst and they know anything else would be anti-climactic. No amount of anthrax in the post or bombs in bus depots can live up to the images of two passenger jets colliding with the Twin Towers in New York. Besides, when it comes to bus depots the terrorists might be doing us all a favour: I've never seen one yet that didn't need redecorating.

How long can the media and the FBI expect the public to remain in a high dopamine fight-or-flight mode, when they keep giving us pictures of nothing happening? Those grainy black and white photos, reminiscent of the ultrasound photo of my firstborn in utero, of fuzzy targets hit hard in Afghanistan are a titch passé. However often Dr. Kissinger says, "We will prevail," the terrorists, I suspect, know there's nothing we can do to match the spectacular visuals of September 11th. If war is theatre, we've been mightily upstaged. By cave-dwellers, no less. It was live, too, for a few moments, anyway. After that we got the same shot over and over again until it began to lose its impact — the way a good phrase becomes a cliché from overuse — and the television stations scrambled to find something else, *anything* to entertain us. That is, shock and horrify those of us who have become so saturated with shock and horror it's made life a farce, and in dubious taste at that.

The night the bombing began in Afghanistan I was with my family, eating Thanksgiving dinner at Long Beach (the Vancouver Island, not the American one). We had no television, but my mother had brought a transistor radio. The only station we could get was an American one — a call-in talk show. "The only thing I know," the host said to his caller, "is that tonight, all the lights are on in Las Vegas."

I thought, they just don't get it, do they? And then last night on the news, mall profits are back up to "pre-attack level."

Life is returning to pretend-normal. God/Allah is in his/her heaven. Malls are making money and all the lights are on in Las Vegas. The terrorists, in a physical sense, have been and are long gone, though they continue to enjoy a celebrated afterlife-style in our collective imagination.

They could have been, those people, a kind of terrible solution.

"Ratio of number of US soldiers killed by hostile fire since 1990 to the number who have committed suicide: 1:5." — my New Year's email-greeting to friends this year culled from the latest Harper's Index.

One of my foreign correspondents — a survivor of both the Korean War and the Free Speech Movement at Berkeley, replied: "The military counts suicide of its personnel (or people) as a friendly fire incident. Much like the family Christmas I experienced this year. Fights over 1) money, 2) money, 3) love. Christmas at the front-line hospital . . . "

Waging peace, whether we be military personnel or civilian casualties — seems more angst-making than war. "Peace is hell" cries the headline of October's feature article in the *Atlantic* (which, needless to say, went to press before 9/11): "Why keeping a few thousand heavily armed, seriously bored soldiers in Bosnia strains the whole US army." One hopes America's Current War has provided troops with an escape from the pressures of boredom.

When I am bored, I wage my own jihad against the careless use of language that works to the advantage of those who wish us to remain uninformed. Truth may be the first casualty of war, but clarity and plain talk have been tried before a secret military tribunal and had their death warrants stamped by Dubya quicker than he could say "Make no mistake about it . . . "

"We go forward to defend freedom and all that is good and just in the world," gushes Bush, repealing the corporate alternative minimum tax, resulting in gifts of 1.4 billion to IBM, to whom Hitler also granted political and monetary favours. (He used IBM computers and tailor-made software to track down Jews; IBM also designed the systems that kept the railways smoothly transporting millions to death camps, and provided software to ensure every punishment and torture in the camps was recorded and organized up until the moment of death.) "We value the right to speak our minds," Bush dictates, signing an emergency order setting aside the principles of law and the rules of evidence. "We will not falter and we will not fail," he philosophizes. "Our ultimate victory is assured." To paraphrase Stephen Leacock, anyone forced to listen to this kind of rhetoric will admit that even suicide has its brighter aspects.

Since the destruction of the World Trade Center in New York, the rest of the world has held its gasping breath waiting to hear some intelligent discourse, hoping the sad events would teach Americans something about their own history — the consequences of their specific alliances and actions — not just the way to pronounce *mujahideen*.

"Operation Enduring Freedom" sounds catchy and important as long as we ignore history and the origins of words. "Endure," according to my *Shorter Oxford on Historical Principles* is a verb, meaning to harden, to make callous. It also means "to suffer without resistance, submit to, tolerate" as in "For how can I endure to see the evil that shall come unto my people (Esther 8:6.). "Enduring" was originally a preposition, which meant, simply, "during".

As far as "operation" goes — most of us have suffered at least one such invasive procedure, and lived — providing we didn't insult the anaesthetist.

The meaning of "freedom" hasn't changed much over the centuries: exemption or release from slavery or imprisonment; exemption from arbitrary control; independence; and (lest we forget) civil liberties.

Put another way, Operation Enduring Freedom is nothing but a procedure by which we tolerate or become callous and hardened by our release from arbitrary control. Clear as mud but it covers the ground.

One thing is also clear: America's Most Recent War is an illiterate one. To declare war on "terrorism", an abstract noun, is much like sending the Airborne to conquer lust or annihilate the sin of pride. A war against an abstraction can never be won or lost; it simply endures.

Americans these days, I read, are scurrying to broaden their vocabularies, though how much longer they will be able to afford the luxury to learn (a single fighter plane costs the equivalent of 80 million textbooks) is a further troubling question. Some of the most frequently queried words on Cambridge Dictionaries Online last fall were *muslim, succumb, perpetrate, debris, retaliate, anthrax, and terrorism.*

"Dear World, I am leaving you because I am bored," wrote the British actor, George Sanders, in his 1972 suicide note. "I am leaving you with your worries. Good luck."

My New Mood summed up, in a cluster bomb shell.

FUCK AND RUN

The United States has been likened to the guy at the party who gives everyone cocaine and *still* can't get anyone to be his friend. So — what is it about our American cousins that makes the average apologetic Canadian apoplectic these days?

For starters, we don't like their national pastime of invading countries whose regimes they (selectively) take exception to. When Donald Rumsfeld coined that bitter soundbite "shock and awe", he could have been alluding to songwriter Liz Phair's "Fuck and Run" — a far more apt description of American foreign policy, from where I stand my ground.

Michael Moore is one brave desperado who has come out in public to denounce his country's "fictitious president". My many other courageous American friends despair even more than the rest of us do — the success of the utterly wicked policies of their government, the terrific venality of everybody else who sees Iraq as one big gas station. The blind boneheaded stupidity of the drooling terrorists is at least comprehensible in human terms. No doubt Osama bin Laden will be the ultimate winner of the American war in Iraq, since the guerrillas and other revenge-seeking Iraqis will enroll automatically in his ranks. "We have only the minority of Americans who voted for the little Bush to blame for an endless morass, which we didn't need to enter for any reason of national interest," my fed-up friend from Berkeley writes. "O I cannot for the Christ's sake go on. Canada looks pretty good right now."

We don't like their double standards. CNN showcases photos of Iraqi POW's with their faces pushed in the mud, then gets their knickers in a twist when Iraqi TV shows the "humiliating" head shots of Americans in captivity. I doubt whether these soldiers, barely old enough to vote, were feeling humiliated; they look too shocked and terrified to be pondering abstractions. Humiliation is what Rumsfeld & Co. have the luxury of indulging in. They promised this war was going to be nasty, brutish, and short. Well, so far there's no end in sight.

Now America has targeted Iraqi television stations to be blown off the map — an attempt, I suppose, to teach those Arabs some manners. This is something else about American diplomacy the rest of us don't like.

We also don't like the patronizing way they try to spare us from the truth. In the last American War (as the Vietnam War is called on the other side of the Pacific) we saw gruesome photos by independent journalists who risked their lives to show the world that war caused excruciating pain. The Bush Administration has 500 journalists travelling in tanks shooting pictures of more tanks slouching towards Baghdad through that relentless Iraqi dust. (A heads-up: find a more scenic country to liberate next time. Those desert scenes are, quite frankly, getting old, and none of us are particularly awed by those night shots where everything looks green, either.)

We don't like the way they treat what NRA spokesman Charlton Heston refers to, in Michael Moore's *Bowling For Columbine*, as their "ethnicity problem". In the American War the draft meant the children of the elite, the wealthy, and the politicians could be called to enlist — another reason why that war ended as relatively quickly as it did. The babes-from-the-woods who are now "playing" in Iraq are not the country's future leaders taking a term off from Harvard or Yale to stop the perceived threat of terrorism: they are poor, they have no future and — just like the American prison population — many of them are black.

We don't like their regime, the one where the majority of Americans never elected the Man Who Would Be President. The Iraqi soldiers are not just fighting for Saddam Hussein any more than we would be fighting for Jean Chretien if we were invaded by belligerents who wanted our resources and believed a regime change would improve our status quo. We would be fighting for our country, our pride, our flag. We would be lying in ambush behind one big, human Canadian Shield, dying to rise up against anyone who tried to take what, for better or for worse, belonged to us. Who can blame the "irregulars" in Iraq for not "playing cricket", for fighting technology with the only weapons they have left: human duplicity and a pocketful of rocks? What's left for them to do but hide their antiquated Kalashnikovs beneath white rags of surrender?

Finally, we don't like *America*'s weapons of mass destruction. Besides, if those smart bombs are as clever as they're cracked up to be, why don't they turn around and go home?

DARING TO SPEAK

My doctor recommends I quit reading non-fiction. It gives me "ideas" he says — unhealthy ones. Non-fiction, in his opinion, includes newspapers; I argue that this is debatable. Besides, reading the newspaper is a morning ritual, along with forcing a fistful of anti-depressants down the inside of my throat: it sets the tone for the day. And, I insist, I'm a columnist — it's my job to know who has been murdered, elected or convicted by mistake, not to mention the latest creative ways my fellow British Columbians have come up with to destroy our ballots for the referendum on First Nations Treaty Negotiations.

"Ever read a book . . . ?" my doctor asks. I wait for him to continue. "About a guy who writes for a newspaper, like you. In the end he goes to Amsterdam and gets himself euthanized. By mistake."

I don't dare ask how you get euthanized by *mistake*. But I take his advice: cancel the rag, buy Ian MacEwan's novel to read on the treadmill at Lady Fitness. I last a week — I'm even plotting a new column on a politically neutral subject — why my washing machine eats socks — until I get to the end of *Amsterdam*, the part where the new editor decides to revamp the paper.

It's time, he says, they ran more regular columns — they're cheap and "everyone is doing them." He suggests they hire someone of low to medium intelligence — possibly female —

to write about, "well, nothing much. Goes to a party and can't remember someone's name. Twelve hundred words."

Other ideas for columns are — can't work her video recorder, her first grey pubic hair, can't keep her tongue out of the small hole in her tooth. And here's the one that really hits home: always gets the supermarket trolley with the wobbly wheel.

Fiction, it seems, can make a writer squirm even harder than what passes for fact. I decide it is time to stop obsessing on the missing socks in my wardrobe and write bravely, instead, about something big and important — some morally neutral virtue, like, say, courage. Eight hundred words.

But first I have some catching up to do. I drive to the corner store and buy the morning paper.

If you are like me and have been living under a news blackout for health reasons, you too may be surprised to hear that four Canadian soldiers have been killed by the same frequent flyers who bomb the citizens of Iraq and Afghanistan from high altitude gun platforms, up there in the realm of the divine. "You don't count the dead, when God's on your side," Bob Dylan sang in one of his earliest anti-war songs. For the same reason, retaliation isn't an option for *us* — because the fellows who killed our countrymen by mistake are, like God, supposedly on our side. To have your body collaterally damaged by "friendly fire" adds deadly insult to deathly injury. No laser-guided bomb, especially one with your name on it, is friendly, unless the spin doctors have contrived to contort the meaning of "friend", as they have twisted "cowardice" and "courage".

Susan Sontag was the first writer with the courage to say it in print: if the word "cowardly" was to be used, she wrote, in the *New Yorker*, a week after September 11th, it might be more aptly applied to those who kill from beyond the range of retaliation, high up in the sky, than to those willing to die themselves in order to kill others.

For daring to speak, she was vilified in the American press; even if she was right, the consensus went, she had spoken too soon. That is, before the insurance corporations had had a chance to cash in on Manhattan's catastrophe and raise their rates to offset their personal losses.

"Whatever may be said about the perpetrators of [September 11th's] slaughter," Sontag wrote, "they were not cowards." If we'd been fortunate enough to have had cowardly hijackers at the helm, the Twin Towers would still be reaching for the sky. "It is better to be a coward for a minute than dead for the rest of your life," as the Irish proverb goes. For our own sake, and for the world's, we can only hope that most terrorists are cowards who don't dare act on their beliefs, who spectacularly lack "the courage of their convictions" and who won't easily be persuaded to commit suicide for the pleasure of causing others pain.

Make no mistake. Without cowardice any one of us is capable of resorting to terrorism as a pro-active way of life. Can't work your video recorder? Always get the supermarket trolley with the wobbly wheel? Praise the Lord, and pass the ammunition.

BABY CHOKES TO DEATH WHILE WHEELCHAIR MOM FORCED TO HAVE SEX WITH ASIAN GANG AND OTHER NEWS OF THE WORLD.

"Sure the world breeds monsters, but kindness grows just as wild, elsewise every raped baby would grow up to rape," Mary Karr writes in *The Liar's Club*. But we humans have a knack of forgetting the kind, and the good: the bad packs more of a punch.

If it bleeds, it leads. Nothing bleeds redder, hotter blood than a crime story — the closer to home, the bloodier. And wherever you find bad blood — anger, rage, or violent behaviour — you'll find the press, out in force. The news can be ugly, and ugly, while it sickens us, also entertains. Who cares about the 5000 planes that land every day, without incident, in Canada? But one that crashes and burns with 365 "souls" on board will fuel headlines for days.

It's the American (and by proximity, Canadian) paradigm: the selling of fear. Television networks, especially, know how to promote everything from the destruction of America's twin economic status symbols to a break-in at your local 7-Eleven. They're skilled at hanging around, waiting for the next newsbreaking tidbit, chatting up the man-on-the-street — even interviewing each other if they are desperate enough — replaying old footage of police lights blinking outside a Paris tunnel. Hunting down a sniper's second cousin twice-removed, or the deaf and blind neighbour of a serial killer, or an estranged wife who can provide photographs of the Unabomber trying to light the family barbecue: who would want it otherwise, and why get off the couch? "Here we all are living more or less happily ever after within the virtual reality provided by a news and entertainment media that can reconfigure death as a sales pitch for a weapons budget, an insurance policy or a face cream," writes Lewis Lapham, in a recent *Harper's*, possibly the most intelligent voice in the American press these days. If a journalist is morally double-jointed enough in this media circus of vicious competition for ratings, readers, and revenue, he might tumble upon a bitterly inarticulate victim who gets his sound bites of anger second-hand through the newspapers and talks about feeling — what else? *Violated.* Hapless victims of crime, thanks to the media, have become the new royalty of the court system.

An example: a young girl taking time out from a baseball game is murdered in the park behind the bleachers. A tragedy has occurred. Suddenly the tragedy becomes a photo-op on the 6:00 news — strangers place flowers and teddy bears at the site where her body was found. Weeping neighbours say it's a senseless murder (show me a sensible murder, or even one that makes sense.) Angry relatives on the courthouse steps, months later, will vow to change the laws.

If the alleged perpetrator (or "perp" in police circles on television, which makes him sound like the pervert they wish him to be) is caught, he risks being convicted by the press before he goes on trial. He is diabolized, referred to as a "creep" or a "scumbag" on talk-back shows. Meanwhile, the victim is angelicized; she has her name and identity obliterated, too. The media now refers to her in prayerful tones. Who among us could not be roused to anger by the unholy image of a dirtbag perp defiling a heavenly angel?

What is the media's job — to lead public opinion or report on it? There are some who argue that the press simply "trafficks" material without exercising moral judgement, the result being that journalists are ignoring — perhaps even crippling — the natural social instinct to distinguish between right and wrong.

Is journalism's claim of objectivity a front for morally irresponsible coverage? Or is moral judgment the role of the reader/viewer? The Fox News Channel in the US encouraged its newshounds after September 11th, to "tap into their anger and let it play," its chief executives proclaiming that "morally neutral journalism is now inappropriate."

In my darkest heart I sometimes wish my husband had waited until September 11th, 2001 to get wired on heroin and cocaine, rob a bank, then shoot at the police who pursued him through Beacon Hill Park in Victoria. His mug shot would then not have appeared above the fold on the paper's front pages all across the country, his "fall from grace" would have been relegated to the bottom of the back page next to a cure for balding. No such luck. He chose a slow-news day that turned into a slow-news week that lasted for months, and same thing, six months later, when his trial began in December.

I don't blame those who work for the papers or the television shows: no point shooting the messenger. Many of them are my friends and colleagues — we have worked together on numerous documentaries and commentaries and columns over the years. But when my husband agreed to be interviewed by one national paper (because the reporter was someone who had come to dinner at our house) I had desperate calls from the rival paper, a young woman in tears because her job was on the line. I found myself, as a writer, in the odd position of feeling responsible for these journalists' careers and states-of-mind. Never mind that my own world was in pieces, that my children were devastated and had lost their father — I was on the telephone trying to cheer up reporters on the verges of nervous breakdowns — all over one-ups-manship, and who got first dibs on the story of my husband's decline and fall.

When the state — the courts, the police, the criminal justice system — is a core player instead of a community — that is, when all are vested interests are in an adversarial process (lawyers vs. prosecutors, police vs. probation officers, prisoners vs correctional officers) — a community has no chance to heal. We are kept apart, made to take sides, and the media's response is often to sensationalize the event, to milk it for all it's worth until some other more current act of anger takes centre stage. Healing — tolerance, kindness, compassion — does not make good copy. Anger rules.

Anger, rage, hatred: these intense, negative feelings serve a purpose in that they feed our need for instant gratification. Loving kindness takes time, and so many people have invested so much of themselves in their anger, they can't seem to let it go. The causes for this anger are deep-rooted and various: personal, primal, intimate. We live it, seek it out, thrive on it, get high on it, and are ready to lie down and die for it.

The media's job is to keep the public informed; news is supposed to be informational, factual, unbiased. Their job is not the organization of anger. Anger will not bring us peace but destruction of ourselves, of one another, and any chance we may have of a future together on this battered and bartered planet we, for the time being, call home.

THE WORLD AFRESH THROUGH PAUL BERNARDO'S EYES:
JUSTICE IN THE NEW MILLENNIUM

The Jew being chugged away to Auschwitz, the nigger on the chain-gang, the queer in the closet, the spic, the wop, the wog: as we enter a new millennium having learned to shed the prejudices of our forbearers, and love our neighbour unconditionally — no matter what his race, religion or sexual persuasion — the criminal is becoming Public Enemy #1, the only minority left to hate.

If trends continue, we can expect to see mandatory castration of sex offenders, lobotomies for addicts, and public canings for children and the mentally ill. Sometime in the future we may hear more Canadians clamouring to have the death penalty reinstated, the institutionalized "magical" solution to a problem we return to when all our knowledge and technology fails. Capital punishment has never done more to deter crime than the Aztec human sacrifices did to keep the sun burning in the sky. Will we remember this in the new century?

In the late 1990s when Canada's most famous serial killer, who had served fifteen years of his life sentence, decided to further outrage the public and apply for early parole under the faint hope clause, the cartoonist Adrian Raeside drew a noose: "The Only Loophole Available to Clifford Olsen." But why stop there? In the new millennium, when state-sanctioned murder becomes *de rigeur*, the least we can do is

SUSAN MUSGRAVE

give condemned men and women the right to choose which form of capital punishment is best suited to their personality — lethal injection, gas chamber, electric chair, hanging, or the firing squad. Pro-Choice, if you like, with a twist.

For criminals who can't make up their own minds, or those with multiple or non-existent personalities, the government will provide a handbook. In this "Guide to Capital Endings", the personality description would come first, followed by an appropriate Final Solution:

1) You're very committed — to work, friends and relation-ships; when the going gets tough you're always there: hanging
2) You're aggressive, crave adventure, live for the moment: electric chair
3) You're a little unsure of yourself, never quite certain what you're looking for: lethal injection
4) You've got a big heart, love everything on earth that lives and breathes: gas chamber
5) You're nurturing, impulsive, a little preachy, but get a bang out of everything: firing squad

In the not-so-distance future, other civil rights, too, will be extended to Canadian prisoners — the right to die, for instance, in a smoke-free environment. Corrections Canada's policy should become one of zero tolerance: no last requests for a cigar or a Player's Light. We might go even further and decide to air condition the death chambers during the summer months, to make it more comfortable for everyone.

Canadians can look forward to a time when all executions will be televised, and would be well-advised to buy stock in the networks doing the televising. Public executions will make investors a ton of money — what with instant replays and summer reruns.

American law has, in the recent past, forbidden the execution of a person who is insane, but, in the new millennium, Canadian law will become pro-active. To determine whether or not a person is sane enough for execution, she will first need to be examined by a psychiatrist. He will ask a series of questions — if the prisoner has ever believed she was a secret agent of God, what century we are in, and the name of the current prime minister. Three strikes and you'll be out: that is, you'll get to sit it out — until such time as you come up with the right answers, and "mental health is restored".

Who among us will ever be sane enough for execution?

The unborn, in utero, perhaps. This brings to mind the age-old question of Young Offenders: by the year 2020 the courts will deem all juvenile delinquents properly eligible for execution before they reach the age of majority. But, as a safeguard to prevent widespread carnage, every child between the ages of thirteen and eighteen will be sent to a "finishing school" to be verbally and physically abused so that by the time they are released they will be demoralized enough to have no energy left for criminal pursuits.

And what about Old Offenders? Those sex-and-septuagenarians who've spent a lifetime in and out of jail because of poverty, addiction, child abuse, and there having been no Young Offenders Programs for them in their formative criminal years of the 1950s. Do we want to end up like the United States with an aging inmate population where more prisoners during the next twenty years will die of heart attacks than from the electric chair, gas chamber, and firing squad put together?

Perhaps some of our incarcerated seniors on Death Row (the name "Death Row" will be upgraded to reflect more progressive times, and will be known as the Health Alteration Clinic) could be persuaded to take "early execution" in exchange for the opportunity to "give something back" to society and become organ donors. That way, parts of these offenders, in the twenty-first century, can start being useful. Such a program, albeit a non-voluntary one, became popular in China in the 1990s, where the still-living organs of executed criminals were harvested and transplanted into more needy, and wealthy, recipients. Who among us, as our own organs begin to fail, will not jump at the opportunity to have Clifford Olsen's heart, or to see the world afresh through Paul Bernardo's eyes?

A few bleeding hearts will protest about the "morality" (if such a word still exists in the dictionaries of the future) of a business that relies on criminals' organs for raw materials. Others will say one organ is as good as the next, providing the donor has led a drug-free, celibate life. And yes, no doubt demand will begin influencing supply. That's business. If this business also feeds an insatiable state killing-machine that leads to more and more executions every year, that's *big* business.

Instead of focussing our anger on those in society who are already most diminished, we have a chance, in the new millennium, to act out of compassion and understanding. In another, oft-quoted cartoon, Pogo says, "I have seen the enemy and it is us." Through our fear and hatred criminals will only become something much bigger, more frightening, than what they already are. Men. Women. Like me. Like you.

THE MAD SEX LIFE AND DEATH OF PRINCESS DIANA

Every time I hear Princess Diana referred to as the "Queen of Hearts" — a title that must make the Queen of England feel even less loved — I think of the nursery rhyme written, once upon a time, as a political allegory:

The Queen of Hearts, she made some tarts
All on a summer's day.
The knave of hearts, he stole those tarts
And took them clean away.

I have no idea how that rhyme might pertain to Princess Diana's life, anymore than I can imagine a good reason for her death, but I do know this woman — who gave grief a human face — stole the world's heart, a world now more full of weeping than she will ever know.

Most people will remember, for the rest of their lives, what they were doing when they heard the news: my brother-in-law was at the drag races, watching cars crashing into one another on purpose; I was lazing in bed and my husband brought me the Sunday paper with its headline, DIANA DEAD.

My second reaction — after disbelief — was envy. What a romantic ending — to die speeding through Paris in the middle of the night with your paramour. It's the stuff dreams — and tabloid sales — are made of. In life, as opposed to romance, though, there can't be anything romantic about dying in a twisted heap of metal, even if it was a Mercedes.

But romance was always what Princess Di meant to us; we grew up believing fairy tales had happy endings. There is the beautiful and good princess, Sleeping Beauty, who gets short shrift from her relatives, then is rescued by a prince who braves the brambles to awaken her with a kiss. Snow White is banished, then poisoned, by a jealous Queen, and finally awakened by love's first kiss as she lies in state surrounded by dwarves. And, of course, there is "Cinderella", the tale of the good girl triumphing over spite and envy, simply by having small feet and being kind to mice. They all get their princes in the end. They had to; there wouldn't have been a story otherwise. Death and marriage, as Nancy Miller points out in *The Heroine's Tale*, have been, traditionally, the only two possible ends for women in fiction, and they were, frequently, the same end.

In *Writing a Woman's Life*, Carolyn Heilbrun says, "Women have long been nameless. They have not been persons. Handed by a father to another man, the husband, they have been objects of circulation, exchanging one name for another." When Princess Diana broke free of her arranged marriage, something in all of us cheered her on. Then she died, too suddenly, in a crash — a Thelma and Louise ending, as if the only way out for a headstrong woman is down — over a cliff or into a one-way tunnel. One wishes there had been other alternatives for Princess Di — not just marriage and/or death.

There's no bringing her back to life now, though the press so far, has performed everything *but* that miracle. There isn't an angle that hasn't been covered, or photographed, about her death or her life. The clincher was Michael Valpy writing in *The Globe*: would Princess Di be getting all this attention if she'd been fat?

YOU'RE IN CANADA NOW . . .

I confess, my thoughts had led me along other, sadder tracks. But he's got a point — if the Princess had been less fit would she have been able to wear those cheeky Versace originals with such verve, or hats with the same panache? If she'd been fat would there have been cameras trained on her hemline at every turn, waiting for her skirt to be snatched up by the wind? Even after her death the shots of her on television started at her ankles and worked their way up to her hairdo.

Roseanne Barr, another kind of celebrity, when asked what it felt like "at the top", replied, "I weep every day. In my limousine." Those of us who can only afford to weep in Honda Civics or Ford Escorts have to wonder: does weeping get any easier behind tinted glass?

It's a bit late for newsagents to start pulling copies of tabloids headlined "Di's Sex-Mad Life" from their shelves; it is bolting the door after the house has been robbed. Sure enough her photos will grace the covers again soon, with Elvis and Marilyn Monroe, photographed by heaven's paparazzi.

Diana touched people, everywhere. Even when she didn't touch them physically, she left a mark, as in the case of a Victoria woman who "almost shook hands" with Princess Diana on her last visit to Vancouver. When this sort of non-event is newsworthy, how can we blame photographers for trying to shoot the world's most photographed woman topless at St. Tropez?

Which brings me to the question of the "tasteless last photographs" many papers are, sanctimoniously, refusing to publish. Why should pictures of a dying woman trapped in a car be any more tasteless than those (taken by a hidden camera) of her exercising, or sunbathing naked? Now that we've been told the pictures exist, but that we can't see them, they are like forbidden fruit — all the more tempting. I don't buy *The National Enquirer* but I'm not above peeking through a copy (hoping no one will notice) to catch up on the latest Titanic Victim Who Speaks Through Waterbed while I'm waiting in the check-out line to pay for groceries.

The paparazzi — *paparazzi* has become a household Italianate along with *ciao*, *cappuccino* and *fettuccini alfredo* — were doing their job: shooting to feed our insatiable appetite to know what it's like to weep in a limousine — or to die in one — instead of in our Hondas or Fords. And some part of me needs to see it all — the good, the bad, the shocking, and the ugly, to look into this dying woman's eyes in her last sudden moments — for reasons, as if maybe she can tell us something about the darkness we're all headed for.

We hope to see, in her dying light, some kind of resolution, some kind of peace. Maybe we won't find it. Maybe we need to face that possibility, also.

CANADIAN PSYCHO

The Professional

I've always believed it's a writer's job to shake up the status quo. My teachers used to tell me I had "the wrong attitude". As far as I'm concerned, it's the only kind of attitude a writer can have.

I started writing when I was in the fourth grade. Horse stories with tragic endings. War Glory, the black untamable stallion who has come from behind and is being ridden by the book's heroine (only she can master him) falls and breaks his leg crossing the finish line. He has to be put down. I set my tale in Ireland and all my characters spoke with a brogue — because my teacher, Peter Seale, was Irish, handsome, and I was secretly in love with him. I wrote epics for him because I just knew he had nothing better to do in his life than go home after school and read my tragedies while his wife peeled potatoes. I admired him, too, because he was a rebel: he didn't "follow the curriculum" as some parents complained, and he let me spend the whole day writing my compositions because, he said, "that's what you're good at." He wrote his comments on my work in bold Italic script. "Is this your own work? If so — 10/10!"

I'd been a straight A-student all through elementary school. I won medals for coming first in my grade. It wasn't until I hit junior high school and discovered boys that I lost interest in bunsen burners, Canadian explorers, and working out answers to questions such as, "Which ocean has the most water in it — the Atlantic or the Pacific?"

I started listening to Bob Dylan. Real life, I decided, had to do with human rights demonstrations, smokestacks and factories — none of which we had in the city of Victoria, where I grew up. But I had an imagination and a romantic streak. I wrote poems set in ghettos in Chicago, odes to drowned cigarette butts in cups of cold coffee. I called my poems "Ode to Existence" and "Futility #16 in Blue". I knew one thing, though: I felt a lot less futile after having written a poem. In fact, poetry made me feel like existence might not be as futile as I had made it out to be in the poems which made my parents think I should see a specialist. I don't think they could bring themselves to say the word "psychiatrist" in those days.

When I was at school "Canadian literature" was an oxymoron. Taking my cue from what I'd read at home (my parents had *Tennyson's Collected Poems*) and what I'd studied at school, I wrote poems set in English fields of daffodils. In Grade Eight, I penned a series of rhyming couplets about Jackie Kennedy visiting JFK's grave by moonlight, and won a prize. I was awarded with a copy of Shakespeare's *Much Ado About Nothing*. I've always wondered if the teacher who chose this book was the same one who taught us about irony.

Teachers played an important role in my development as a writer. When I was in kindergarten I had once been sent outside the classroom for the crime of laughing (my friend tickled me), to sit it out on "The Thinking Chair". In Grade Nine, I kicked an apple core in line and spent my detention in the library. The message I got throughout my formative years? "Thinking, and books, are bad."

I learned to make the most of my punishment, and started reading the library books, which is more than the librarian must have done or else Irving Layton's *The Bull Calf*, full of four-letter words, would have been pulled from the shelves.

Layton made love and sex, where the nights are long here in Canada, sound *more* exciting than a stroll along the Seine or a trip to the top of the Empire State Building.

I didn't feel qualified to try writing about sex, but after reading Layton I became more experimental. I wrote poems full of words I couldn't pronounce — "Evolutionary Obsequies," for example. The poem itself rolled off the tongue a bit more easily. "Life is like a candle. Blow it and it's gone."

I went to the kind of high school where kids were given sports cars for failing Grade Eleven. I felt I had more in common with Count Dracula than I did with the other girls in my class, aspiring cheerleaders with blonde hair and ortho-dontically altered teeth. My parents, of British extraction, believed it would be vain and unpatriotic to have my teeth straightened, that crooked, pointed teeth would help form "character". I became withdrawn, anti-social, and I never smiled, which gained me a reputation as a serious poet, a poet of "gloom and doom who writes of the darker side of life". While the cheerleaders shook their pom-poms I skulked beneath the bleachers writing "Vampires should be liberated . . . "

In 1967, the year I left high school for good, my boyfriend — whose father was a Math professor at the University of Victoria — gave me a hit of acid (LSD) for a Valentine's Day gift. Even though I could spell *evolutionary obsequies* I had never taken an alcoholic drink in my life, nor smoked pot, or even tobacco.

Once a week for the next six months I dropped acid in an artist's studio in the Uplands district of Victoria, close to where I lived. Christina was from Santa Barbara; her parents were millionaires, she went to a private girls' school, and she had everything from a chauffeur-driven Rolls to her own armadillo skull. I was happy when I was high, but the depressions I went through in between acid trips got worse and worse. Eventually, after I had run away from home a number of times to live the hippie life on Vancouver's 4th Avenue, I had a small nervous breakdown and my parents had me committed to a psychiatric institution.

I spent my days writing and reading poetry. Even though I had never been able to write anything while I was high, and not much when I was coming down, now that I wasn't dropping acid once a week I had to do something with my mind. As Gracie Slick of the Jefferson Airplane said in "White Rabbit", "Feed your head". I had fed mine — overfed it — and now I was waiting to make sense of what I'd ingested.

A few years ago my friend Christine's sister organized a reunion at their old house, and invited those of us who had survived the 60s. There, pencilled on the studio door, were four lines of poetry:

Is there in this field of gypsys
And the emptiness of their wandering songs,
Is there a favoured child of beauty
Bruised and irremediably bereft?

"That sounds familiar," I said. Crowbait, my old boyfriend — the one who'd given me my first hit of acid, who now sold real estate and used his Christian name, James, said, "You wrote that."

"Bruised and irremediably bereft?" I detect now a smattering of Plath (the "bruised" part) — but "irremediably bereft"? Thirty years later I still can't tell you what it meant.

CANADIAN PSYCHO

A writing habit, like a drug habit, is one you have to develop as early as possible, before you get other ideas about growing up. Having a full-blown habit means you won't be faced with a lot of confusing choices about what to do with the rest of your life.

Before you try to write, you should read. (Why bother getting a life of your own when you can live vicariously through a writer who has made at least one genuine suicide attempt, has a substance-abuse problem and smokes a packet of cigarettes a day?)

Here are a few reasons why reading is not a complete waste of your time:

1) READING PROMOTES INDEPENDENT THINKING. If you were lucky enough to have parents who read to you before you were old enough to open your mouth, hit back, or dial 911, you can become anything you want — a sadist, a masochist, or anyone in between. Violence begins at home, and nothing helps hone your developing criminal mind like having nursery rhymes shoved down your pint-sized throat. In the average collection of traditional nursery rhymes you'll find enough blood and horror to jump start any little law-abider down the tortuous path of independent thinking — allusions to mass murder, of choking to death, death by devouring, cutting human beings into bite-sized pieces, decapitation, squeezing, starvation, boiling to death; cases

related to the severing of limbs, or the desire to have a limb severed; whippings and lashings; allusions to maimed animals. If you want more, read *Mother Goose*.

2) READING IS ECSTASY, ONLY LEGAL. "I hate to advocate drugs, alcohol, violence or insanity," said Hunter S. Thompson, "but they've always worked for me. (Originally Thompson included "reading" on his list, but some illiterate editor X-ed it out.)

3) READING WILL HELP YOU LET GO OF THE CULTURAL MINDSETS YOU HAVE LEARNED ABOUT SEX. If you don't read you'll never know about the "good parts" in Henry Miller's *Sexus* — the one, for instance, where the guy sticks a cigarette in a woman's vagina and makes her inhale while he walks her around the room like a wheelbarrow. *That*, I tell you, got my Grade Seven class hooked on reading.

4) READING IS SUBVERSIVE. Only by reading the book will you be qualified to discuss, intelligently, the sex and torture scenes in *American Psycho*. There is something in your local library to offend everyone. Check it out.

5) READING KILLS TIME. "Cheerio, see you soon." Epitaph on gravestone.

I started reading as an escape — from life, my parents, my imaginary friends, the mental hospital — but especially from school. I started writing for the same reason. And to get attention from boys.

1) WRITING WILL GET ATTENTION FROM THE OPPOSITION SEX. In Grade Seven (same year as *Sexus* turned us all into bookworms) I sent my crush a Valentine's Day Card from every girl in the class — and, from the ones who "liked" him, multiple orgasmic Valentine's. From me, he

got nothing. He chose me to be tied up with (in the three-legged race on Sports Day) because he thought I was "sensible" (he disapproved of girls who chased boys). Since then, writing has always got me what I want. Pretty much.

2) WRITING WILL MAKE YOU FREE. In Grade Eight I began forging notes from my parents demanding that I be released from all forms of Physical Education, especially gymnastics, because of the possibility I might contract a rare developmental brain injury. My forgeries were so successful that the word got around, and soon everyone was paying me to excuse them from Math, Science, English, and, especially, Guidance. I made enough money to invest in a shipment of Orange Barrel Acid, which I sold to the kids who had skipped school in the hopes of finding a less excruciatingly boring way to waste a spring afternoon.

3) WRITING MEANS NEVER HAVING TO SAY, "HELLO, SAILOR . . . ". One of the best things about being a writer is that you don't need a respectable wardrobe. When I was in Grade Eight I started going steady, skipping school to make out, writing poetry and listening to my boyfriend play "The Times They Are A'Changing" on his guitar in a field of itchy grass — until the principal called me to his office. He said if I continued down this slippery slope there would be only one career opportunity left open to me in the future: prostitution. Even then, I knew this wasn't in the cards for me. I didn't want a job where you had to work with other people.

Besides, hooking requires a wardrobe of sorts, even if you do have to keep taking it off; writing means you can keep your clothes on, and nobody expects you to have a body anyway. You don't need to be in shape to sit hunched over your Power

Book all day, occasionally moving your fingers to lift a coffee cup as far as your lips.

The best thing about writing is that you can do it from your own home, and you never have to talk to another human being, unless you are totally sick, or desperate.

4) WRITING CAN BE A CONSTRUCTIVE ALTERNATIVE TO CRIME. Why bother vandalizing a telephone booth or going to Serial Killer School when you can avoid earning a criminal record by writing about the crime you didn't commit instead, and then collecting royalties? All it takes is a wallop of imagination; a smattering of personal experience, passion, chutzpah; and the ability to write in clear four-letter-word sentences and then you too can be on the BANNED BOOK list in all god-fearing public schools across the continent.

5) WRITING WILL MAKE YOU SO FAMOUS that autograph hounds will hand you pen and paper under stall doors in public washrooms; strangers will stop you on the street to ask "What have you written that I might have read?"; if you die young or rob a bank, your book will finally start selling and go out of print.

6) WRITING CAN BE REVENGE. If your lover dumps you, you can write about it. You can give the slut he's oozed off with a rare communicable sexual brain disease, make her breasts leak silicone when she lap dances at Billy's Topless, or even better, endow her with no breasts at all. You can even be kind, and write about how having your heart eaten while you were still alive converted you to vegetarianism and how you have accepted Christ because you want at least one sympathetic male figure in your life. Writing well is the best revenge.

7) THE ZEN OF WRITING. Why do I write? Because it isn't there.

I have come here, to my beautiful, shining, windy house on the Queen Charlotte Islands, to do — nothing. Nothing includes finishing my novel as soon as I finish cleaning and canning the coho that practically jump out of the river into my sink; harvesting and pickling the ubiquitous sea asparagus ("You can't let them go to waste," my environmentally-friendly neighbours, Aviva and Harmony, say when they stop by with a hemp sack full of chanterelles for me to dry) making salalberry jam (before the bears get all the berries); and putting the final touches on my daughter's log cabin (walls, windows, roof, etc.) — a project she started in the summer but didn't have time to finish — as soon as I find a mechanic who hasn't gone fishing and can install a master-slave cylinder in my Toyota so I can drive to the Co-Op and buy a litre of So Nice Soyganic for the increasingly hot flashes. Oh, and did I mention the cat, Bitz, who adopted us in August and, when I had to go back to Sidney to get my daughter settled in school, climbed the highest hemlock on the property?

Bitz has been meowing in the tree for nine days straight and she won't back down. "You're a writer. I can't wait to read the story you get out of this," Jude, with HUG A LOGGER on her T-shirt, says, when she picks me up hitchhiking to Masset, and I tell her my woes.

"Whenever Insane Fuzzball – that's my little shit for brains cat, eh — goes up a tree, Dwayne, he's my better half — this week, anyways,eh — he says to me, think about it, you don't see a lot of cat skeletons in trees."

I try to hang on to this vision, that of not having seen a lot of cat skeletons in trees, but it doesn't last. You don't see skeletons in the branches, but I'll bet if you poked around in the dirt at the foot of most trees you'd find a surfeit of lovely bones.

In Masset I stop by the Volunteer Fire Department hoping someone there might come to my aid, but the doors are locked. "I came back to the islands to get away from it all and instead I am going to pieces over Bitz," I lament to a clerk behind the desk at the Masset Council Office. The clerk doubts whether the firemen will be any help. "Psycho cats aren't their jurisdiction."

Before dark, when I go out to make a last attempt to lure Bitz down for the night, I can no longer hear her plaintive cries. I pour myself a glass of fortified Soy Beverage, further fortified by a shot of Jamesons, and sit by the fire remembering what I read about people in total despair not bothering to cry because they don't believe crying will make any difference. When we shed tears it's a sign we still trust somebody cares.

Later, tired of lying awake listening to the silence in the trees, I get out of bed and seek help on the Internet. I search for "how to rescue cat stuck in tree" and find endless dead-cat-up-a-tree-joke sites and an unhelpful Chinese proverb, *Don't climb a tree to look for fish.*

By morning I've made plans. I dress in loose-fitting clothes, tie my hair back with an elastic, and don a carpenter's apron. I take a hammer, a fistful of nails, and a dozen foot-length boards I'd used to shore up a sand bank, climb to the top of the extension ladder, and begin nailing the boards to the tree.

I hadn't counted on so much sand falling in my eyes or my neighbours turning up to help me feel worse. These back-to-the-earth-mothers are the type who, when they cut firewood on the beach, sweep up the sawdust and take it home to burn in the wood stove so it won't pollute the environment. I inform them I am building a stairway to Bitz because the tree limbs are too rotten to hold my weight. "How do you think the tree feels about getting nails hammered into its carcass?" Harmony asks.

I abandon the idea of a ladder and move on to Plan B, ascending onto the slippery-sloped roof of my house with a baggy of salmon under one arm and a cedar plank under the other. I arrange the salmon tidbits on the end of the plank, then lay it from the roof across to the highest branch I can reach, hoping Bitz will take the bait. I don't recall a Chinese proverb saying anything about not crossing a bridge onto a roof to look for fish.

An hour later I'm still on the roof and Bitz hasn't budged from her perch. I'm starting to feel relaxed: I have a better view than the one I get from my office window — no telephone, email, kitchen stove or sink. Aside from the woozy swarm of black flies feasting on my exposed ankles and wrists, it's not a bad place to live. It occurs to me that Bitz might have climbed the tree for the same reason I retreat to this remote island in the north — to get away from it all.

"Are you writing?" my husband asks, when he calls that evening, collect, from down south. My cat has narrowly escaped dehydration (Dwayne, Jude's better half of the week had come by an hour ago, and felled the tree with his Husquavarna) in a hemlock and my husband wants to know if I'm writing?

Of course I am, I snap back. When am I never not?

BOOKSELLERS FILL A MUCH-NEEDED GAP

When Calvin Trillin edited his *Anthology of Authors' Atrocity Stories About Publishers*, he didn't extend his survey to include booksellers. Every published writer has her own collection of sad short stories based on the humiliating experience of searching for her latest, wildly reviewed novel in a bookstore where the average shelf-life of a trade edition is somewhere between milk and yoghurt. "It is true," Trillin writes, "that some books by Harold Robbins or any member of the Irving Wallace family last longer — but they contain preservatives."

While writers have been known to joke that booksellers fill a much-needed gap, many of us moonlight as booksellers ourselves, carting boxes of our books to literary readings. I buy directly from my publishers at the author's discount — 40% off, but after paying for shipping and handling, I usually end up *losing* money.

Last summer I was invited to read, as the warm-up for Michael Ondaatje, at the Association of Writers and Writing Programs Conference, held this April, in Vancouver. I didn't think to take my inventory of books, as the onsite bookseller (a well-respected Vancouver independent) had almost a year in which to order copies for the 4000 eager American conference-goers (and my few diehard fans who always infiltrate from the street).

Michael and I read to a packed ballroom at the Vancouver Hotel; afterwards we were shown to a table to autograph books. Judging from the applause, I'd figured I'd sell a *few* of my books, if not a couple of thousand, but instead I watched an infinite line form in front of *The English Patient*'s famous author.

Then, one by one (I counted — I had time on my hands) ten homeless-looking people approached me with copies of my out-of-print collections, no doubt stolen from garage sales. One, dressed in a well-worn tweed hat and jacket, asked me to sign my first poetry book, on permanent loan from the Vancouver Public Library. (It turned out the hat and jacket belonged to the poet George McWhirter and had been stolen earlier in the evening at a reception; George's wife, Angela, accosted the thief and demanded he give back the clothing, which he claimed to have purchased on the street for twenty dollars.) When the crowd had come and gone, the bookseller came to apologize — due to an "oversight" she had not ordered "enough" copies of my books — the ten copies she *had* got in had been left behind at her shop. I tried, as I lay awake disappointedly that night, to find a positive way of viewing this atrocity. Maybe those 4000 Americans would think I was so popular — like Harold Robbins and the Irvings — that every one of my books had sold out before it even hit the bestseller list.

I should have learned from my previous experiences that booksellers have more on their minds than keeping my books in stock (there are, after all, upward of 100,000 new titles published every year in the English language alone: it helps to recite Stevie Smith's poem, "I am only one of many, and of small account, if any . . . ") and that I should lug my own books to literary events if I hope to have copies available. This doesn't always turn into a mega-marketing success, either.

Last fall I had loaded my half-ton and headed over to the mainland to another writers' conference. At the hotel sponsoring the festival I approached the owner of the independent bookstore, and asked if she'd sell books on my behalf. She sighed, but I persisted, offering her the bookseller's discount — 40% off (which would mean I would lose money — again). She sighed — again; she had, she told me, just been diagnosed with ALS. "Want to know what the prognosis is? Death."

I prepared to slink away with my slim volumes of sorrows (hard to slink when you have a dolly loaded to the gunwales) but she called me back. "Leave them with me. They might generate interest."

When I went to check out, on Sunday, my books had "done surprisingly well" (every copy had sold); I humbly asked for a cheque (I owed my publishers big) and the bookseller said the cheque would be in the mail. A month went by and I decided to send an invoice. I got an email saying the bookseller had died the night the conference ended and the bookstore had gone into receivership, that I would get paid, eventually, right after the banks and the publishers who had jumped in line first.

My books, and the small amount I lost, seemed of little consequence against the bigger backdrop of mortality, and I was grateful for the reminder: I had better get to work — writing books, not distracting myself with the deadly business of selling them.

ONDAATJE ON THE HOOK:
THE POET AS RESTAURANT CRITIC

"It is a true error to marry with poets," wrote the American poet John Berryman. It is also a true error to choose one as your dinner companion when you have to recall the event with any clarity the next day.

I am both blessed and cursed that The Deep Cove Chalet, near Sidney, on Vancouver Island, is the closest restaurant to my house — less than a couple of miles away. It's too easy, on nights when I don't feel like "salmon again", to get in the dinghy and row around the point and have Pierre cook up a little sea bass with veal stock, or cod in puff pastry. On the other hand, when I first started eating there, twenty-five years ago, I weighed forty pounds less.

Pierre Koffel's reputation is legendary. Everyone has a story about him. My favourite is the one where he swims out, with a bottle of champagne, to a sailboat full of celebrities that has just dropped anchor, climbs aboard dripping wet, pops the cork, then dives overboard and swims back to the kitchen.

Besides the rich and famous, there are the regular locals like Air Canada pilot, Paul Stenner, who keeps his own jar of mint sauce under the counter at the bar (Pierre does not serve his Rack of Lamb with mint sauce, nor does he do Soup 'n' Salad.) Whenever I've taken writers to dinner, Pierre has read their books. The last time Matt Cohen and I ate at The Chalet, Pierre gave us a bottle of good red wine some snob had returned saying it was off (it wasn't) to take home with us, and we went out rowing and got swept away by the tide. We didn't care; we had the stars, free wine, and the feeling we could live forever.

There is a timelessness to this place; you feel as if you have escaped from the getting and spending world onto the set of a play by Anton Chekov. In the winter evenings there is always a fire burning in the hearth. In the summer, you can sit outside on the terrace, whale watching over the Saanich Inlet. Pierre's wife, Bev, does the voluptuous flowers arrangements inside, and there's always some new painting on the wall, or sculpture to look at in the garden.

But, as magnificent as the atmosphere is, both inside and out, it's the food that keeps people coming back. My last visit was on a warm July evening; Patrick Lane and I sat outside under a grandfather maple, discussing martinis, and having some. Once the sun disappeared behind the mountains we moved inside to a table with a view over the lawns that slope down to the sea. A cormorant sat on a floating log, drying its wings, silhouetted against the darkening inlet.

We weren't brought menus which meant Pierre was going to surprise us. As an appetite-whetter we were served small bowls of delicate savoury broth with a sprinkling of herbs, croutons, and the first chanterelles of the season. With this came a bottle of Cotes de Saint-Mont 1998 which Patrick said, "has a plum quality with the edge of a knife." At least, I think that's what he said. By the time I had fished out my notebook he'd forgotten his exact words — very important when it comes to nailing down the qualities of a fine wine. He thought he might have said "an icy edge" but I'm sticking to my story: a plum quality with the edge of a knife. *I'm* the one who has been asked to take over *The Globe and Mail*'s restaurant critic's job this week, while she is on hiatus.

Our waiter, noticing our almost-empty glasses, tops us up, and I notice we've made a serious dent in the bottle before we've even finished the pre-appetizer course. "Nice and tight," Patrick declares, of the croutons, "like a woman. Keeping the tension in the crouton is hard work." Then, after a reflective pause. "I should be writing this!" Little does he know. He is.

Next comes a Dover sole so delicate it could slip through your breath (my line, not Patrick's.) "This sole looks like Ondaatje on the hook," Patrick says, not to be out-done. At least, when I look at what I've written, it *appears* that's what he said. It could have been "Ondaatje on the book" but that wouldn't have made sense. Unfortunately, not much is making sense by this point. The evening seems to be slipping from our hands.

Finally, Patrick says something normal. "This is the best Dover sole I've had in my life!" I can tell he means it because he has even eaten the skeleton.

That was the last note I took.

I know we had a second bottle of wine, and that it was red: I meant to make a note of the name. At that point I decided to pace myself, which meant making sure I drank glass for glass with my companion so I would get my share, and as a result I am unable to remember the nuances of what we had to eat. I can safely say that Pierre can cook lamb so it melts in your mouth; you don't even need teeth in order to eat it.

They say a good writer is one who can make you drool and your gastric juices begin to ferment by describing the smells and tastes of a memorable feast. I'd like to be able to describe our final course in the kind of elegant language a sober restaurant critic might use, ("then came an apple upside-down tart with warm thyme-infused honey") but by this time we had dropped the last vestiges of the discreet charm of the bourgeoisie. Dessert was something with puff pastry, poached pear, and blackberry sauce. No little seeds that get caught in your teeth, either. It was yummy. I would have asked for a second helping but that might not have been . . . professional.

It's unusual to blush when alone, people say. But a friend of mine says he was alone driving when he first heard Leonard Cohen's song, "Light as the Breeze", and felt his face turning crimson. "Then my wife later told me that when you listen to Leonard, you are not alone."

It seems that almost everyone has an intimate relationship with this poet.

Cohen's lyrics have never just been lyrics — they are a way of life. They have infiltrated our souls and our homes and become part of the heartbreaking decor. Who can peel an orange or sip China tea without dreaming of rivers and envisioning Leonard in another man's raincoat wandering by?

Way back when I first fell in love, "The Stranger Song" was "my song". All the men I have known ever since have been dealers (drugs, emeralds, gold bars, you name it) although none of them, like in the song, needed a manger. More like a manager. Still, a girl can dream. And crank up Leonard Cohen, whose voice can make you feel just about anything — from drawing on the insides of your arms with a Gillette Super Blue to making another stab at love — over and over again.

I've met Leonard, in the flesh. (For the record, that's as close as we ever got.) We were both young and unattached. Well, he was. That night, anyway. *Death of a Ladies Man* had just been released and I was in Vancouver promoting a collection of love poetry, *A Man to Marry, A Man to Bury*. My publicist invited me to a gathering in honour of Leonard Cohen.

We arrived early, and my husband (I was married but, as I say, not attached) cornered Leonard to talk to him about the rigours of law school. I left and went out on the verandah to look for the moon.

Secretly, of course, I hoped Leonard would follow. My publicist had told me he admired my poetry, and I imagined him caressing a dog-eared copy of my book and telling me, "I always read your poetry. At night. In bed."

I watched him come towards me out of the house. And when he spoke to me in that voice full of broken whiskey bottles and desire, he said, "I *really* like your husband."

Was there life after *Death of a Ladies Man*? I lived. But I buried (metaphorically, of course) the man I'd married and Leonard went to Los Angeles to live on Mt. Baldy with monks.

I remarried and moved to Ontario to be Writer-in-Residence, which was where I was sent for an ultrasound. The results were grim: I should come back, the doctor said, in six weeks, to see if my tumour, the size of a Christmas orange, had metastasized.

Whose tape was I playing in the car on the way home from that lugubrious appointment? Leonard Cohen's. "The Future". I drove, with tunnel-vision, into that intense white light that seems to surround everything when you are reaching for the sky, not just to surrender, but for divine intervention.

They say a near-death experience is like a near-sex experience — nothing like the real thing — but when you believe you are close to death, as I did, and you listen to Leonard Cohen's version of the future over the Christmas season, whilst pushing away from the gravy so you can still fit into your coffin, it can be bleak. At night I lay in bed imagining my organs being strangled, one by one, by this starfish-type sarcoma, to the strains of "Closing Time".

I wanted to live to be a hundred and wear something tight, but if I didn't make it, and died at forty instead, I insisted this song be played at my funeral. "She listened to that song a lot towards the end," my bereaved husband would tell the small but interested group who came to pay their last respects, and to get at the free booze and cheese.

Of course my intimations of mortality were premature (wrong diagnoses). I lived to blow the candles out on my forty-first birthday, and many more afterwards.

What's next after near sex and death with Leonard Cohen? One thing I know for sure: with Leonard there's always more.

I've been playing his *Ten New Songs* these dark wild evenings as I drive out to the prison where my husband lives, singing right along to "A Thousand Kisses Deep." Just the way the word *kisses* slips from his lips: I can't say it makes me blush but I definitely feel . . . less alone.

A LOST CLASSIC

I found John Coulter in the Shannon airport, in the west of Ireland, in May 1979. He lugged an antique typewriter plastered with CNR stickers, and I offered to carry it for him. We sat together on a plane to Toronto; he was eight-nine and going home to settle down, he said, in Canada.

In the years before his death, at the age of ninety-six, I visited him whenever I was in Toronto, at the apartment he rented on Avenue Road. John, a playwright, had known the days, as they say in Ireland, and also the writers. He pronounced Yeats to rhyme with "beets", and told me James Joyce had stolen his walking stick, which was now on display in a Dublin museum. He intended to get it back. On one visit, after he had read some of my poetry, John loaned me a fragile little book called *The Name and Nature of Poetry*, by A.E. Housman. This essay, which I have quoted from over the years — in my own essays and book reviews — captured the essence of what I had always understood about poetry, but had never been able to articulate.

Poetry is not the thing said, but the way of saying it, Housman wrote. "Even when poetry has a meaning, as it usually has, it may be inadvisable to draw it out."

"I hear you write poetry. Modern poetry. That's annoying," an elderly aunt (twice-removed) shrieked at me, when we were introduced. Housman's essay provided me with the perfect retort, one I've used often when confronted by an aggrieved family member or stranger claiming not to understand my poetry. First of all I quote Coleridge (as quoted by Housman) who said poetry gives the most pleasure when only generally and not perfectly understood, that perfect understanding will sometimes almost extinguish pleasure.

If that doesn't satisfy, I try this:

"The majority of civilized mankind do not possess the organ by which poetry is perceived. Can you hear the shriek of a bat? Probably not; but do you think less of yourself on that account? Do you pretend to others, or even try to persuade yourself, that you can? Why be unwilling to admit that perhaps you cannot perceive poetry? Is it an unbearable thing, crushing to self-conceit, to be in the majority?"

Most people will be stuck for an answer.

But then there are the professional critics, the ones who get paid, who want to know what your poetry means to mean.

Meaning is of the intellect, Housman says; poetry is not. He feels poetry is more physical than intellectual — causes a shiver down the spine, or makes the whiskers on the chin stand up (he must have believed civilized women did not possess the organ by which poetry is conceived, either). The best poetry, I think it can be agreed upon, horripilates.

Why can mere words have the physical effect of pathos? "I can only say because they are poetry, and find their way to something in man which is obscure and latent, something older than the present organization of his nature," Housman says.

I made a few notes in my journal (looking over them now, I see the ink has begun to fade) then returned the book to John, who said, "I should leave this to you." And, in an unexpected way, of course, he did.

"WHEN WE GET THERE CAN I SMOKE?"

"I don't know how they keep this train on the tracks," says bill. We pull out of London's Paddington Station. "In two weeks I will be chopping wood in the Cariboo."

I've left my life, a marriage gone to sleep with a glass of wine in its hand. I have no one to run back to, no place to hide. "In two hours I can smoke," says bill.

We've been travelling for days — the trains, the lonely stations. In Norwich we saw a church that had been bombed by a zeppelin; in Oxford we read to a college of gay Quakers. In London, last night, we went to a party at David Hockney's flat and bought tickets to see "Camelot" and then have dinner with Richard Burton, but didn't go.

Instead, as bill would say, we raged into Wales. In Cardiff we compare parasites, take in the Impressionists and Gwendolyn Davis' fake bronzes, including *The Kiss*. We meet a Trotskyite in a wine bar, eat fortune cookies under a photo of the Grants of St. James (land grants, mostly). I get "Romance is iffy."

bill isn't convinced; he's been told Cardiff is a hotbed of vice. He finds The Private Shop, whose windows had been whited out to keep the public from looking in, and an array of potions to make love last. Longer. It is International Rugby Day in Cardiff. "They talk on the telephone with their drawers down," we hear someone say. Romance is looking iffier.

In Coventry there is fisticuffs in the hotel at night. I dream I am too refined to eat sugar. bill always asking me, "Are you feeling festive yet?" In Coventry I get a wake-up call: "Your cold breakfast is coming up."

We wake up cold in Yorkshire, too, with stone pigs stone cold at the foot of our beds. Mrs. Jackson, the landlady, says the cold is piercing. "We don't have summers," she says.

At the Church of Spiritual Healing we climb the blue staircase, kneel before the blue bear on the altar, the starfish on the altar cloth. bill gets a message from a Hindu in a green robe through Mrs. Peel, the healer, whose people were taken in caravans from their land of red rain, long ago. Mrs. Peel says there is a question in bill's life.

I get a message on my palm, a red wound, a stigmata. bill sees it and touches it — a miracle! bill will be cured, too: no more parasites! I light a prayer paper and a little cloud goes up. "Blessings can go through walls," bill says.

In Heptonstall we go looking for Sylvia Plath's grave, and find a blue suitcase, the weeds in lovely riot. The suitcase matches the blue shoes bill always wears, the ones he's worn out with so much travelling.

At first we couldn't find her, the cold was making it hard. "Maybe she did it to get warm," bill says. That could have been part of it.

At Lumb Bank, a writers' workshop, we meet Damian who's been questioned by the police because he looks like the Yorkshire Ripper, and Colin, who's written two books called *Panic* and *Asylum*, and who questions bill's syntax. Later in the village there are fireworks and bill dances away over the hills, dances back with the young girls who have been awakened by shooting stars. White moths come out of the hedgerows, drawn to the light around bill's body, settling on his hair, on his face, all over his clothes.

I don't know how we keep this train on its track, with all the distractions we have to face daily. Glasgow, Dundee, Edinburgh, Leeds. A newspaper headline in Newcastle reads SEVEN YEARS FOR SEX BEAST and I think of Camus': "A single sentence will suffice for modern man. He fornicated and he read the papers."

Romance is consistently iffy. I don't know how we keep doing it — behind the walls of hotel rooms, pubs and guest houses, B&B's, the small smoky rooms where we read our poetry. I dream bill and I have an adobe in Arizona. "I heard some good news today," says bill. "We come this way but once."

Then over the sea by British Airways to Paris (bill asks "when we get there can I smoke?") where we read at the Canadian Embassy. We visit a bookstore that has been bombed by extremists, and laugh with a firebreather who wants me to go with him. Afterwards, bill says you have to wait two years in between major relationships, so I don't leave; I stay. At the Louvre I watch bill flick a booger onto the *Mona Lisa* to see if it will set the alarms off. It may still be there, bill's booger, to this day.

"Is everything brilliant?" bill asks, when, on our last evening in Paris, the sirens start playing our song and the man bleeding on the sidewalk asks for a smoke, a light. "Got flame?" he says, in darkness. bill gives him his last cigarette.

And flying back to Vancouver the next day, "You are My Shining Star" coming in through our headphones, our faces messy with tears, the terrible parting yet to come. bill going back to chop wood in the Cariboo, asking "Are you feeling festive yet?; me thinking I might head down to Colombia to drink orange juice and talk about emeralds.

"Brilliant," bill says, when I tell him.

HOW TO BRIBE A JUDGE

Until I met the Honourable Justice James Clarke of the Ontario Superior Court of Justice I'd only had one other experience with a poetic judge. Unfortunately it was my former husband who inspired some of his worst poetry. Charged with importing thirty tonnes of marijuana from Colombia, my better half had brought his disabled freighter ashore on Vancouver Island and, in the morning, when the law arrived, he headed for the hills. He stayed there for a week, dining on frog, which he cooked over a fire. The judge, who left his poetry behind for the court clerk to contend with, penned: "I found a frog, near a bog, under a log, in the fog . . . " Even though James Clarke, too, must often while away his hours listening to lawyers and experts gurgle on about flood plains, geodetic elevations, and hydraulics until he feels like sentencing "every windbag in the courtroom for the crime of boredom" — he has never written anything as forgettable as that.

I met Jim in 1996 when he enrolled in a writing workshop on Lake of Bays, in the Muskoka. He brought with him an attractive humility and a bulging manuscript; his poems had me weeping one minute and laughing out loud the next. He wrote with wry humour on just about every subject from bicycle theft to stolen love. When it came to the law and the plight of his fellow man he proved an old saying, "Even as there are laws of poetry, so is there poetry in law." His was poetry that let us peek under Madame Justice's blindfold, giving us a rare glimpse of her concerned, but very human face. His sixth book, just published and seductively titled, *How To Bribe A Judge*, might be — if it were to end up in the self-help section of a bookstore, in these litigious times — an inadvertent bestseller.

It's hard not to take comfort from the persona of "the judge" that Jim Clarke has created for himself in his poetry. He remembers being a victim himself — a boy, falsely accused of stealing a few coins. The more he protested his innocence, the more he was disbelieved. He sends a warning to us about young offenders who will be "delivered back to you," older and deadlier in less than three years. In numerous poems the judge sees victims on all sides, and has the wisdom to know there is not always an unwavering solid line between guilt and innocence.

That he knows there is more to every human tragedy than gets reported in the newspapers is perhaps why he is able to feel pity for the clumsy thief who leaves his fingerprints as a calling card, "whose simplicity/makes us want to forgive/like Jesus/his artless mischief." He understands that prison, the granite underworld full of broken lives, is a place "where love belongs to a lost language." As well, the judge has the ability to laugh at himself. His first day in court he dons the trappings of office, the black robe and red sash, then marches into the crowded courtroom, "anxious to create an impression of decisiveness," and trips, landing on his nose in a tangle of silk. Elsewhere he writes of receiving a letter, signed "John Q. Public," informing him that without question he is the worst judge in Canada and that if he had even a sliver of self-respect he would resign. "Laugh heartily at all his jokes even when they're incomprehensible," he advises, in the title poem.

"Quote with boldness from his old decisions, no matter how dull, irrelevant or wrong."

Life has not always been just to Jim Clarke, himself. Poetry is what has helped him cope ever since that not-so-long-ago Palm Sunday when his wife of twenty-five years left the house, drove to Niagara Falls, and dropped away into the mists. Although kept private, it wasn't kept secret; many of James Clarke's poems approach a need to understand, a desire to somehow occupy that four-second fall from life.

In spite of there being " . . . nothing we can plead or do/ in our defense except/describe the way we came," James Clarke shoots straight from the hip and from the heart. "Without appearing obsequious finish every sentence with 'My Lord,'" he further advises. Finally: "never appeal his judgments."

Jim Clarke's path, and I daresay that of most of the men and women who stand before him in court, could not possibly have been more divergent. Yet, each of his poems is a reminder: no matter how different the experiences from which we examine and judge our lives, the human heart beats on, and to a common beat.

YOU WILL DIE ROARING

There is no point in sending abusive letters to writers these days. It only encourages us.

"Dear Arse-Bollocks," begins one reader's missive to the Irish writer, Joseph O'Connor, each time his column appears in a Sunday newspaper. Joe eventually responded to this "lobotomized virago clearly in need of severe treatment": "Now, how one can be both dear and arse — not to mention dear and arse and bollocks, simultaneously — would be a matter of speculation to some people, particularly to students of biology and contortionists . . . "

Most hate-mail writers I hear from have a number of problems in common. Besides needing the obvious kind of help, they need editing. "Alan Fothringham (sic) says Susan Musgrave will never get hemeroiuds (sic) because (pronoun omitted) is such a perfect ashole (sic)," is one of the more literate messages I've received smeared across a facsimile of my face. When I say *smeared* I am using the word in its broadest possible sense. The poor man must not have been trusted with a pen in the padded room where they keep him chained up.

On Friday I returned from a week of self-imposed isolation on the Queen Charlotte Islands. A writer friend, who once published a series of poems on the sex lives of vegetables and received death threats in the mail, met my plane. When we got home, I checked the messages on my answering machine, one of them being from the Security Branch of Canada Post. They had mail for me "of a sensitive nature".

A young man with a cold told me the letter had aroused suspicion because the sender had chosen to compose his letter on the *outside* of the envelope: "You still around? Whatever happened to that trip to Holland to have thyself euthanized? Do consult your partner-in-crime about a coke dosage. Your constant whining is quite passe. Suicide? Artistic? What a *pathetic* person? you must be."

You don't hear "thyself" (second person archaic) used much anymore. The interrogation mark after "person" gave me pause, too. Was the writer expressing editorial uncertainty, as in "Saint Fracas (456?-458 A.D.) had a short but raucous childhood", or simply following the rule that a question mark should stay at the end of an interrogative sentence that is part of another sentence, as in "How had this dreadful suspicion arisen? was the sensitive question on everyone's lips."

The congested young man at Canada Post had not opened the letter because the contents (unlike the words which were everybody's, including Canada Post's and CSIS's business) were a privacy issue, he said. I gave him the go-ahead and held my breath while he removed the black electrician's tape that had been used to seal the handcrafted envelope.

"There's nothing but a piece of Kleenex inside," he sniffed, sounding almost disappointed. Until I reminded him that anthrax spores could be invisible and not to blow his nose into the tissue until it had been sent to the laboratory to be analyzed, and a DNA sample secured.

My friend, who had been eavesdropping, said the social leper (who lives near Ottawa, a fact Security had ascertained from the postmark) probably had relations of a personal nature with the Kleenex. Family members speculated that the tissue might have been contaminated with anything from smallpox to common human spit.

When I consulted my partner-in-crime, who seldom lets me down, he said all of us were digging too deep. "It's to blow your nose into," he said, practically. "After you've finished whining."

Whining, by the way, is another problem hate-mail writers have in common. It's the verb they all drop when straining to describe the kind of work a writer does, whether it be expressing an opinion, exploring an idea, or having an original thought. They throw it up, adjectivally, also, as in, "You still have not taken my advice and dropped that whining piece of New York Jewish dreck you are married to," a letter the American writer John Gregory Dunne, whose wife, Joan Didion, is a WASP from Sacramento, gets every time he publishes a piece.

Still, Dunne maintains wackos are important to writers, because most of us have an interest in aberrant behaviour. The nut who insults your spouse, questions your parentage ("if any"), and predicts your future ("you whine your last by Tuesday"), opens a window onto the "real" world.

I won't hazard a guess about what goes on behind closed windows in the real world, but I do know there's an awful lot of literary talent out there, waiting to be unleashed. "You are a curse and will die roaring with your legs in the air," writes another of Joe O'Connor's detractors. "All I can say," O'Connor responds, "is you never know your luck."

HOSTAGES FOR COFFEE

The Penitent

RAISING THE EXHILARATION CONTENT
OF THE UNIVERSE

They're mad, bad, and dangerous to know. They are portrayed as "likable rogues" of the "good badman" type, "gentlemen of spirit", rebels with a cause. They live outside the law and, in doing so, turn the tables on the nature of society. "Outlaws, when they succeed, raise the exhilaration content of the universe," writes the American novelist, Tom Robbins.

There's an intriguing psychology at work in our love-hate relationship with criminals. References to criminals as "dirt", "slime", and "scum" pervade the media and everyday conversation. We repudiate them, but we admire them, too, and we rationalize our admiration in a number of ways. The outlaw may be seen as hero, defying corrupt authority in defense of the "higher" cause of social justice. We may sympathize with him as an individual at odds with society, one against many. Individualism is one of the tenets of Romanticism, and one with universal allure.

Novelists, playwrights, and folk singers have perpetuated a romantic outlawry tradition in which the bank robber has been awarded the most glamourous image of all. The old-world charm of the so called "Gentleman Bandit" still appeals; the charismatic rogue with a quick *bon mot* and a social conscience is a sexier figure than the potbellied monopolist living in a moral shadowland. Banks, we further rationalize, rob us every day. I've heard countless people say it: "If I could commit one crime, and get away with it, it would be robbing a bank."

The legendary outlaw, despite his crimes, retains his humanity. Jesse James, for instance, is more often portrayed as a clean-living church-goer, faithful to his wife, than he is a vicious psychopath.

Jesse's sense of humour is mythologized as much as his saintly deeds (he was famous for rescuing bankrupt widows and damsels in distress.) He reverses the shoes of his horses to lead pursuers in the opposite direction; he assumes a disguise and a bumpkin's demeanor to join a posse searching for himself. While real-life outlaws do pull tricks to escape capture, folklore embellishes their stories for an audience that evidently enjoys seeing the hunted outwit the hunter.

Perhaps our pursuit of money has something to do with our respect for those who go after it with guns blazing. Our esteem for the hold-up artist is mirrored in the language we use to describe his line of work — beginning with the word "artist" itself. Bank robberies are inevitably "daring" or "brazen". Ever heard of a meek stick-up or a dull heist? I'm sure, given the numbers, there have been a few.

Outlaws are just more *interesting* than inlaws, which may be the simple reason why our society is obsessed with them. Our most popular books and movies are preoccupied with them. They are the ones who do our dirty work for us, thumb their noses at authority, spit into the wind. Outlaws represent an almost childlike freedom we wish we had.

Take the scene in *Butch Cassidy and the Sundance Kid* where Butch takes Etta for a ride on his bicycle as B.J. Thomas sings "Raindrops Keep Falling On My Head". Butch is a threat to orderly society with boy-next-door appeal; it's impossible *not* to like him, especially when his movie role is played by

Paul Newman with those regulation killer-blue eyes. Men look up to him, women fall for him. There is perhaps nothing more appealing than a man who is half outlaw, half good citizen.

Johnny Wisdom is another movie variation on a theme we identify with — an essentially decent man becomes a victim of persecution. When his situation becomes insufferable he turns on his persecutors and makes revenge his *raison d'etre*. He goes on a bank-robbing spree and, when the money's in the bag, he blows up vaults where mortgage-records are kept (easier to be an anti-hero in the days before computers) thereby freeing long-suffering farmers from greedy officials and evil land-grabbers who have the power of the law on their side.

The music score in these bank robbery caper films — up tempo and full of rollicking tones — tells us the bad guys aren't out to hurt us; they just want the dough. A scene in a movie theatre in *Bonnie and Clyde* captures the disparity between the movie world and the bandits' shoot 'em up style. Onscreen, dancing chorines sing "We're in the Money" in a Busby Berkeley production number. In the audience Clyde brags about killing a bank guard — the first of many killings to come. The movie immerses us so deeply in the delusions of its heroes that it makes banks deserving targets, stick-ups a lark, and lawmen bloodthirsty bullies. It takes bullets, at the very end, to snap us back into our seats.

And then there is the ubiquitous banjo by which nearly every car-chase getaway scene is accompanied. "I've robbed 150 banks in my life and never once heard a banjo," my partner, who is the quintessential half outlaw, half good citizen, once confessed.

The paradox remains: how can we, in good conscience, demonize crime as citizens and, as readers and moviegoers, romanticize criminals? We say tut-tut to outlaws during their lives and then, once they are safely dead and time has softened memories of violent eras, name our children and our public buildings after them (the Billy Miner Pub in Maple Ridge, British Columbia comes to mind). We produce fun-heist films of their exploits while doling out prison sentences for armed robbery twice what you'd get for murdering your spouse. The message is discomforting: money is more valuable to us than human life, and the dangerous people we need to lock up are the criminals we'd most like to be — as long as we get away with it.

Outlaws can be a picky lot. Jesse James, a chili head, refused to rob the Lone Star Bank in McKinney, Texas, because his favourite chili parlour was there. Billy the Kid was allergic to dairy products, and the Sundance Kid wouldn't eat an egg unless it was served to him sunnyside up.

As every self-disrespecting gunslinger's moll will tell you, the way to any outlaw's heart is through his mouth. In January 1930 Clyde Barrow, who started his criminal career stealing turkeys, met the ninety-pound, golden-haired nineteen-year-old Bonnie Parker who was "sort of married" to a convict serving ninety-nine years for murder. They formed an odd relationship — he a repressed homosexual, and she a woman of great appetites.

When Clyde's attempts to support Bonnie by playing the saxophone failed, they turned to robbery. They knocked over grocery stores, luncheonettes, and a few small-town banks. They killed at least thirteen people, eluded police, slept under the stars, and lived on peanut-butter-and-jelly sandwiches.

On May 23, 1934, near Gibald, Louisiana, Bonnie and Clyde were killed in an ambush; a posse fired 187 bullets into their bodies. Clyde had been driving in his socks and Bonnie had one of her sandwiches in her mouth.

Sam Bass (1851-1878) began his career when he and two cronies took their loot from some "easy rustling" and opened a whorehouse in Deadwood, Dakota Territory. Described as "the most degraded den of infamy that ever cursed the earth", the brothel did a thriving business.

But Bass and his gang (including Canadian Tom Nixon) could not be accused of having had beginner's luck when they drifted into the hold-up trade. They robbed the Deadwood stage four times from July to August 1877. Their total loot consisted of fifty dollars and seven ripe peaches. (The gang split apart over how to divvy up seven peaches four ways.)

These days most crooks can cook. And they love to eat. They eat while planning crimes, after committing crimes, and, when nothing's happening, they eat while waiting for a crime to happen. They eat as if they're going to the chair, like Donald Snyder, who arrived on Death Row weighing 150 pounds, and then turned glutton, gobbling huge portions, always demanding seconds. His plan was to get so fat he wouldn't fit in the electric chair. He fried weighing 300 pounds.

Mobsters are big on sauces — lots of butter and heavy cream. The theory is: any meal could be their last so it better kick anus. Big Jim Colosimo (1871-1920), overall crime lord of Chicago , provided protection for a couple of whorehouse madams; when a problem came up Big Jim would arrive juggling jars of spaghetti and his own home-made tomato sauce. While the girls gave him the 411, he would make them a pasta they couldn't refuse. Then he sat down with them to "swallow the clothesline".

CRIMINAL LINKS: Al Capone had plates of steaming sausages delivered to his hotel room every day. But there were also times when the gangster liked to do his own cooking, as well as his own killing. At one dinner party he hosted, thirty of his guests had more than just their digestive juices stimulated. Big Al served his homemade sausages-on-toothpicks, devouring a dozen or more himself while he made an impassioned speech on the subject of gang loyalty and team spirit. To drive home his point, he produced a baseball bat and beat to death two suspected traitors who, the moment before, had been unsuspecting dinner guests.

DEATH BY GARLIC: John Scalise and Albert Anselmi, two cutthroats who became known as the Mutt and Jeff of the late 1920s underworld, brought to Chicago the old Sicilian custom of coating their bullets with garlic. They mistakenly believed that if their shots were not true, the garlic would kill the victim by causing gangrene to set in. Though their combined IQs were less than blood temperature and their medical knowledge somewhat off-target, the same could not be said about their homicidal prowess.

"Prime Minister of the Underworld" Frank Costello (1891-1973), did a short stint in the Atlanta Pen. Frankie continued to enjoy his steak "ebony on the outside, claret on the inside" just as he'd always ordered at his favourite restaurant. No one ever uncovered the source of the steaks.

THE PARSLEY RACKET: While prisons are notoriously full of crooks, a lot of crime goes on under the table, too. Ever wonder about that parsley garnish you get with every meal you order at your favourite family restaurant?
It started in New York: restaurants were forced to serve parsley with every meal, and even with a number of mixed drinks. As the Mothers and Fathers Italian Association (MAFIA for short) jacked up the price of parsley, some restaurants found their parsley bill running as high as their payoffs to the police.

Since most diners push their parsley aside, a few restaurants began trying to cheat the mob by washing the parsley off and reusing it. But suppliers weren't fooled. A count of tablecloths and napkins by mob-connected laundries proved which restaurants were scrimping on greenery. They were given a warning: a firebombing.

Chances are, wherever you find crime, you'll find something cooking. Ma Butterworth, mother of seven, operated a successful counterfeiting ring right out of her own kitchen; the "Cucumber Bandit" ate the evidence afterwards; and two Toronto pickpockets squirted ketchup on unsuspecting targets before leaving them penniless. Then there's the Great Train robber who got caught by leaving his fingerprints on a cookie jar.

Harvey Milk, the murderer of San Francisco Mayor George Moscone, pleaded guilty by reason of insanity, invoking the now-famous Twinkie Defence. His lawyer said Milk had gorged on sugar-loaded Twinkies, which induced a rush of temporary insanity.

FAST FOOD: Two men were arrested and charged with theft after making off in their getaway car with a statue of Ronald McDonald from outside the chain's restaurant in Canonsburg, Pennsylvania. A ransom note demanding 150 hamburgers, 150 milkshakes, and one diet soda to go, was delivered to the drive-thru window. The note also threatened to melt the clown into ashtrays and sell them to a competing restaurant.

BRINKS BEFORE DINNER: A gang of thieves in Montreal was foiled when one of its members — a man well-known to police — was spotted carrying an armload of take-out food into a warehouse on a Sunday. When the Surete radioed for backup and conducted a search, they discovered a tunnel leading into the main vault under a

Brinks depot. But the tunnel was bare. The thieves had vanished, leaving behind a police scanner, four cheese pizzas, and sixty million dollars in cash.

YOU ARE WHAT YOU STEAL: A man apprehended outside a meat warehouse in Denver, Colorado, was found in possession of boxes full of inedible rectal tissue, which are used to cure cheese.

While being driven to jail, the suspect learned what he'd stolen. "If I go to jail for stealing 1200 assholes, I'm really going to look stupid," he said, and the statement was used against him at his trial.

Another Oklahoma con-artist launched a suit for two million dollars against Coors brewery, claiming their product had pickled his brain.

It's not just well-known outlaws and crooks who have connections in the culinary underworld. Even Shakespeare was once prosecuted for poaching a deer, and Katherine Hepburn's distinguished career as an actress was preceded by a shorter, more undistinguished stint as a burglar. She stole a pair of crocodile nutcrackers before her life of crime came to an end. The cook caught her.

FAMOUS LAST MEALS: Gordon Fawcett Hamby, executed in Sing Sing in 1920, ordered a lobster salad for his last meal, saying, "At least I don't have to worry about indigestion."

James Donald French, electrocuted in 1966, turned to a newsman on his way to the chair. "I have a terrific headline for you in the morning. French Fries."

As George Appel, electrocuted in 1952, was being strapped into the chair, he quipped, "Well, folks, you'll soon see a baked Appel."

JUST DESSERTS: A California company has brought out Gummy Lawyers, a chewy candy in the shape of a shark. "The shark has become the national emblem of the profession for legal consumers," said a spokesperson. Gummy Lawyers comes with a warning to any sucker who might risk eating one. "Like the real thing, they'll leave a bad taste in your mouth."

THE LAST KISS

Every time I take off my underwear I think of June the 9th. I kissed Stephen goodbye that morning and reminded him to pick up cat food on his way home. "Right after I knock off the First National," he said. A family joke.

It's over five years since I've had celibacy thrust upon me. A year of living, as Butch Cassidy called it, in a state of Single Cussedness. Stephen, former leader of The Stopwatch Gang (famous for making it in and out of a bank in less than a minute and forty-three seconds), had taken heroin for a mistress and spent four minutes withdrawing $100,000 of other people's money from a bank that day. "I could have taken out a loan in less time," he told me later. *That* realization, when it came to him, had almost jolted him back into sanity.

But sanity for Stephen had become sticking a needle in his arm again, shooting up a heroin and cocaine cocktail every fifteen minutes. Still, he wasn't too wired to have a plan. It went something like, "Aha! A bank! Let's rob it." Another part of his fantasy was to take a ghetto blaster into the bank, stick in Pearl Jam's version of "The Last Kiss", then stick the place up while he danced.

On June 9th, instead of going to my office first thing the way I usually do, I polished the woodstove with stove-black, using a bunch of old rags that used to be my favourite pair of Stephen's Joe Boxer's. After the stove was black, and the rags were black, I tossed them in the washing machine. Waste not, want everything, that's my motto. Besides, you never know when the world might be hit with a shortage of rags.

I also had some underwear — a white bra and panties — in the laundry basket and, rather than waste water on two separate loads, I threw these in with the rags and added a cup of Cheer.

Stephen and I have been married for thirteen years but have never found a way of marrying our differences over the management of our finances. When it comes to obscene amounts of money he believes "there is always more where that came from" (i.e. the bank); I *deposit* money and leave it to work for me at a quarter per cent interest per annum.

So on June 9th, while he, disguised as a transvestite Barbie, was at the bank, I was saving rags and dying my underwear at the same time. And after that I went to my office to work on a poem:

LONELINESS

takes the good out of all of our goodbyes,
more permanent than the sadness you know
when your lover drives away having lost
interest in everything about you, especially
your suffering. Love's a blip, a glitch,
but loneliness signs on for the duration,
one gunshot wound to the head is all it takes
to assure your allotted space in today's
News of the World . . .

June 9th, 1999, at one o'clock, I went into the house and checked my machine for messages. There was one, from a pay

SUSAN MUSGRAVE

phone, an unidentified caller: "You may want to do a bit of housekeeping. Stephen might be in a bit of a sticky situation."

My first thought was, "Housekeeping!" Hadn't I just polished the woodstove and done a load of laundry? But then the "sticky situation" bit began to sink in. Any minute now the police might arrive to do the kind of housecleaning your house never recovers from.

I unlocked my front door, though I've heard drug dealers say the police like to break down the door even if you leave it wide open for them, and waited. When I didn't hear sirens, only the sound of my lonely 38D being tumbled dry, I went back to my poem.

The cure for loneliness, they say, is solitude,
trust everybody but cut the cards, take your delight
in momentariness . . .

～～～

At first glance it looks like a fairy-tale castle-hotel: parking lots shaded by endangered oaks, crew-cut lawns, a stone wall running the length of the property. But when you look again you see it's a dungeon, with bars on every window and razor-wire surrounding the yard. The poet Lovelace may have been right when he wrote, "stone walls do not a prison make," but razor-wire doesn't leave a doubt.

Visitors call it Wilkie, as if they feel some affection for the joint, or because Vancouver Island Regional Correction Centre is too much of a mouthful. It was built as a mental hospital at the turn of the century, on Wilkinson Road near Victoria, with two gold-painted lions that lie in repose on either side of the steps leading up to the prison doors. I hand over my driver's license and sign in at the front desk as if committing myself,

· 212 ·

as if shock treatment might be a relief after everything I've been through since Stephen was arrested two days ago.

The papers say I am standing by my man. I'd rather be laying by him, I think, as I start to undress — take off my wedding ring, belt, and sandals — then walk bare-soled through the metal detector. A guard inspects my Birkenstocks, making sure I haven't concealed contraband — drugs, money, or books — between the straps. I ask if I am allowed Kleenex — not that I *plan* to weep, but, if you want peace, prepare for war has always been my motto. He says he will "provide me with something."

My visit takes place "under glass". I feel like a kid again — complaining about leftovers, and my father saying, "What did you expect? Pheasant under glass?" — as I enter the small plexiglass and concrete booth designed by someone with the aesthetics of the sensory deprivation chamber in mind. The walls are off-cream, the trim around the windows a tinned lima bean green. All else is puce, and the graffiti is misspelled: SEE YOU AT THE ALTER BEEFY.

It's familiar decor. Stephen and I were married in prison, in 1986, when he was serving the last months of a twenty-year sentence for bank robbery. He was paroled twelve years ago, almost to this day. But prison is not a place easy to escape, even if they release you. "Nor iron bars a cage."

The guard brings me a roll of toilet paper, and unwinds what he thinks I'll need. The $50,000 a year it costs to keep a man behind bars must not include the price of a box of Kleenex.

STEVE LOVES SUE FORE-EVER is etched into the plexi-glass. I have forever to think about the other Susan who visits the Steven with a "v" waiting for my Stephen with a "ph", but when the door to the prisoner's booth finally opens, the man

I am supposed to be standing beside is not the one standing before me. The guard picks up his telephone, I pick up mine. "He's refusing the visit," he says. Point-blank.

I knew Stephen would be going through withdrawal, so I'm not surprised that he can't keep our date. Part of me, though, feels betrayed. When we got married we vowed to be there for one another, *through sickness and in health*. The one-ply toilet paper, not meant for tears, is soon the size of a spitball in my fist.

I'm trying to leave when I am summoned to the Assistant Director's office. He indicates a pile of papers and asks if I'm familiar with the "ionizer". This machine has picked up microscopic particles of cocaine on my letters to Stephen; my driver's licence, too, is contaminated. Given that my husband's had a thousand-dollar-a-day drug habit for the past six months, it seems likely that my whole *life* would be contaminated.

"We don't want inmates in contact with individuals involved in drug-seeking activities," the official explains, when I ask why invisible drug particles could be a problem. He will suspend my visits if I ever attempt to smuggle contraband to a prisoner.

How could *anyone* smuggle *anything* through plexiglass, over a telephone? I ask. He says, "Where there's a will, there's a way."

~~~

Next time I visit, Stephen has come down, and doesn't stand me up on the other side of the glass,. He picks up his heavy black telephone; I reach for mine.

Some previous visitor has severed the wires, which have been jury-rigged with electrician's tape. Our voices fade in and out, accentuating the lonely long distance between us. He says that minutes before they fetched him for our visit, the wind slipped into his cell. He knew that meant I was there.

I bring him some good news: his novel, *Jackrabbit Parole*, is being reprinted. And my own novel, after eight years, is finally off to the printer's. "It's about a woman visiting a man in prison, so it's timely," I said.

"Well, it's going to be timely for a very long time," Stephen replied.

I reach out to the glass, and see the reflection of my hand rest itself on Stephen's. The SWAT team crushed his hands when they took him down as he was passed out on the couch in an elderly couple's apartment where he had been hiding from the police. "Don't be mad at them," he told me. "It's just cops, they're just doing their job. In Toronto they would have killed me."

My reflection travels up his arm, stutters over the track-marks, and then moves sadly on. I stroke his trembling face. Where there's a will, a way. A way to touch, even if it's *this* way.

Two pheasants under glass. I don't cry until the visit is almost over, and this time I have nothing to wipe my nose on except my T-shirt sleeve.

They lead Stephen away through the puce-coloured doors. I wait to be released, and book my next visit. But when I begin to spell my name for the new guard on shift, she stops me. "I know who you are," she says. "You've been an inspiration to me all my life."

She has taken me by surprise. I hadn't allowed myself to see past the uniform.

"I used to write poetry — at university. We all did. But you didn't stop like the rest of us — we had to get jobs." Her voice drops to a whisper. "I admire everything you've ever done. Except for one thing."

I expect her to say, "Marrying a criminal."

"You know those essays you used to write for the newspapers — about family life? Well, I thought they were trite." She doesn't think domesticity a subject worthy of my inspirational words. As Stephen would say, even guards are literary critics nowadays.

Some days I feel lost, other days life continues without Stephen, though he is here in every grain of wood, every dustball behind the woodstove, every fixed or broken thing. Words are what I know, and that I have freedom in my love. All of him washes over me, like the mystery of wind.

∽ ∽ ∽

A month after his arrest, we are granted an "open visit" in the Visiting Room. Even though we are no longer "under glass", there is still glass, nose-high, between us, and a sign saying PASSAGE OF ARTICLES OR PERSONAL CONTACT "PROHIBITED". Instead of having personal contact we try making as many words as we can out of the word PROHIBITED. *Debt. Debit. Rob.*

It is a humbling experience, visiting Stephen in prison again. But at least I can leave. They keep Stephen Hannibal Lectered in a high-security ward with a bunch of criminally insane garden gnome thieves who steal his mail to get the names of writers who can help publish their memoirs. They are psycho-killers who refer to the Crown as "Satan's Whore Mother".

Stephen was sentenced on December 22nd. The judge gave him eighteen Christmases. Our first conjugal visit is coming up. There will be just the two of us, alone, for seventy-two hours. For the first minute and forty-three seconds, I'll be wearing my stove-black underwear.

HOSTAGES FOR COFFEE

When Stephen first faced having to quit smoking at Wilkinson Road Jail (not because I pestered him every time I visited with, "Have you quit smoking yet?" but because a province-wide ban was being instigated) he decided to write about it. Around the same time I got a phone call. A man with a thick accent: "Sussanah. Do you know who this is? This is John." He added a last name. It was the hostage Stephen was supposed to have taken, along with his wife, last June 9th, after the failed bank robbery and shoot-out in James Bay.

I had called them in June to thank them for being so kind (Cathy, John's wife, had sat patting Stephen's shoulder saying, "God works in mysterious ways," and John rolled him cigarettes.) I wanted to bring them flowers, to have them meet our daughters. Cathy called a few days later to say thanks, but John wasn't well enough to see anyone.

"John," I said, into the receiver, "how are you?"

"I am twenty-five years in isolation in this building," John said. "How is Steve? My doctor, five doctors, they send me home to die. They say to me, "Go home, John, and die." Now I am a well man. I go to park, feed birds. I live another 30 years."

An hour later I was still listening. "The police say my wife not to call you or take flowers. I listen to her but she is like second mother to me. Take this. Brush your teeth. Always direct me like mother to boy. My wife very good woman. Without her I would be dead a long time."

John said he and his wife wanted to come and see me and tell me their story. "Tomorrow."

Now my husband's actions were causing me even more grief: what would I do when John wanted to smoke? How can you tell a man your husband kept hostage in his own apartment, a man who rolled cigarettes for your husband in his hour of need, that this is a non-smoking house? I could picture John saying to himself, "No wonder Steve he desperate man."

Maybe if I *hadn't* asked Stephen to smoke outside, things would have turned out differently. Maybe if my eldest daughter hadn't called him a *loser* when he smoked, and our youngest daughter a *quitter* when he tried to stop, he wouldn't have grown desperate enough to mainline drugs.

A month after being sentenced, Stephen was transferred to Matsqui Institution near Abbotsford for a twelve-week period of induction. He was probed, analyzed, tested, and assessed; he scored 100% on the literacy test and was advised to try his hand at writing. "Journalism, for example," I suggested. "So you make enough to pay for your tobacco."

Desperation (i.e. the thought of nicotine withdrawal) being the mother of invention, he had a working draft by the end of February. He found an envelope, stamped it, and sent it out. Three days later he got his article back, from the Visitors and Correspondence office who screen all outgoing and incoming mail, marked "Insufficient Postage".

That was okay, he told me over the phone, because the ban had already been in effect for several days and convicts in other prisons were rioting and he wanted to rework the beginning. A week later he found another envelope, stamped it with more than adequate postage, then attached a Post-It with "Time Sensitive" on it (big mistake), and a note to the Visitors and Correspondence officer saying I would be coming to visit on Saturday, could I take the article with me?

I made an even bigger mistake. I told the V&C officer the *Vancouver Sun* had a deadline, and that this was, after all, our livelihood. "Everyone loses their livelihood when they come to prison," she reminded me.

Not only could I not take the envelope out with me, five days later Stephen got it back again saying, "Contraband envelope. Use only envelopes purchased from the canteen or those in your personal effects."

The large brown envelope had come from his effects, left over from his stint on a Royal Commission, but it was pointless to complain about the injustice because we'd missed another deadline. Besides, the judge's ruling had been overturned and Stephen wanted to rework his ending. By now I had quit asking, "Have you quit smoking yet?"

It's hard for anyone to be in prison, but for anyone who likes to *communicate,* it's extra tough. There is no email access. Books must be sent directly from a publisher, though the same V&S officer who objected to Stephen's envelope sent a book back to one Vancouver publisher because it was signed by the author, which, she decided, constituted a gift. Newspaper clippings I often included in my letters (we both clip items that may give us ideas for stories, poems, or essays) were returned marked "contraband;" if I photocopied the same clippings they were allowed in.

I got an extension from the *Sun* on the deadline; Stephen rewrote his article once again and sent it a third time. Only by now it was spring break and I had left for the Queen Charlotte Islands, during which time the smoking ban law was overturned, and Stephen was transferred to Mission Penitentiary.

Ten days later I arrived home and found his article waiting for me. I typed it out and emailed it to a friend in Mission. I asked if she could print my slightly edited version of Stephen's article and get a "gate pass" to get it into the prison so he could read it and give his approval.

I left for Montreal. The next time I spoke to Stephen he had spent five days fighting to rewrite his article. "I can't see what you don't like about it," he said. The trouble with email is you can't attach Post-Its. I'd simply wanted him to approve my changes, and he'd got the impression it needed a major rewrite.

At Mission the staff goes out of its way to help visitors feel at home (so to speak). No envelopes have been arrested, no books returned to sender. I know now that when I send Stephen a letter it won't be sent back saying, "Never use slippery onionskin," or "We prefer paper 8x10." My daughter's works of art reach him, without having been ripped apart: they found no heroin under the Hello Kitty stickers she stuck to his Father's Day card, and no cocaine under the red and green sprinkles she glued to his card for Christmas — nothing but lipstick kisses all over the photo of herself she sent for his birthday. But they had to look.

You try to keep your sense of humour, especially when those around you haven't got one. "The way he gets treated around here," I said to one of the more pleasant officers before Stephen was transferred out of Matsqui, "you'd think my husband was in *jail*."

CRIMES OF BOREDOM

After a course of therapy left him "correctly oriented" but bored with life, the writer Graham Greene began to play Russian Roulette. In his autobiographical essay, "The Revolver in the Corner Cupboard", he wrote, "Boredom, for me, went far deeper than love. For years . . . I could take no aesthetic interest in any visual thing at all; staring at a sight that others assured me was beautiful, I felt nothing." Greene would take his brother's revolver, load one chamber, point the gun at his head and pull the trigger. When the hammer clicked on an empty chamber, he felt released from his ennui — for the moment.

"There is only one thing to do when you are bored — learn something," I advise my husband (who is prohibited, for the moment, from owning firearms) on the very rare occasion he complains of finding life in prison a tad mind-numbingly dull.

Boredom, I don't need to remind him, is what put him back behind bars. Like ninety percent of the incarcerated men and women, and many of us on the outside, my husband had learned to turn to mood altering substances when life got too hard, or too easy. The addicted need more and more drugs, which release them — the same way Graham Greene was released — from a life of mostly boring formalities.

Bertrand Russell wrote that at least half the sins of mankind are caused by the fear of boredom. Nietzsche said only the finest and most active animals are capable of it. He also said that God's boredom on the seventh day of creation would be a subject for a great poet to tackle.

John Berryman, a great poet, didn't live long enough (he ended his life by jumping from a bridge) to contemplate God's tedium, but he did write, "Life, friends, is boring. We must not say so." To confess one was bored, his mother used to profess, was to conclude that one had no inner resources.

Prisoners, of course, have resources. They have television: like heroin, it keeps the population subdued and under control. They have librariesand weight rooms; a few have makeshift golf courses (why this incenses the man on the street I'll never know: for me cruel and unusual punishment would be a putting green surrounded by barbed wire where I was expected to swipe at balls with a club for the rest of my sentence: I'd be the first one campaigning the government to bring back the noose) and most have Family Visiting programs where "convicted" families can go and spend three days and nights living together like — what? A normal family?

There is nothing normal about prison. Being barred from all commerce with mankind is boring, even when you are Just Visiting. You don't get phone calls. No email or Internet. No trips to the post office, no surprise deliveries from FedEx. No visitors dropping in. The view through the razor wire, no matter how beautiful, never changes. You can't escape from it to rent a video, or go for a walk, or pick wildflowers. In the cupboard there is the ever-challenging board game, Sorry; on the bookshelf, a TV guide.

It didn't take me long to conclude: in order to survive living in prison — whether it be for eighteen years or three days — one must have inner resources. So on our Family Visits I bring in books and many of the magazines I seldom have time to read at home.

And I learn. On our last visit I learned about an "abdominal time bomb", the aortic aneurysm, after which I developed the precise vague symptoms. I needed something sweet to console me. From my husband, leafing through the same *Utne Reader*, I learned that the bittersweet chocolate I had planned to use in my brownies probably came from cocoa beans harvested by regularly beaten, inadequately fed child slaves on the Ivory Coast.

Not wishing to eat brownies tainted by slavery, I made bran muffins instead, then turned on the ten o'clock news where I learned that forty-six percent of the people living in the city of Baghdad are children, so that if the Americans go to "play" (as one bored soldier from Georgia put it) they will be playing war with kids.

As always, I turn to poetry for solace. "The facts of this world seen clearly are seen through tears," Margaret Atwood wrote, in "Notes Towards a Poem That Can Never Be Written". Boredom, as I read her words, suddenly felt like a luxury, and prison a safe haven in a dangerous world.

WHAT WOULD BUDDHA DO?

Genius is not a gift, said Sartre, but the way we invent in desperate situations. No way we were going to cancel our three-day conjugal visit just because our Food Order got lost. We would live on love — and other couples' leftovers — alone.

As soon as we were alone, I took inventory: one frozen chicken and a two-pound bag of frozen Brussels sprouts. Two trays of ice-cubes. Years ago I read an article that suggested that by applying a fistful of ice-cubes to your partner's testicles at the "right moment", it would prolong his orgasm. Timing being everything, it's one trick I hadn't tried. Yet.

In the cupboard, a plastic container marked GUN POWDER. Stephen insists it is baking powder, but in baking, unlike in sex, I'm not so willing to experiment.

We have potatoes. You can never have too many potatoes, as they said in Ireland during the famine. I begin to work up an appetite thinking of the barbecued chicken we'll have tonight, and those baked potatoes, each topped with a dollop of sweet, melting . . . ice-cubes?

As for the Brussels sprouts, I've never found a use for them in my kitchen. Surely God had some ulterior motive when it came to their creation?

Stephen is peacefully watching mobsters wack each other on TV. I curl up on top of him with a good book: *How to Be a Great Lover*. While the author doesn't include Brussels sprouts on her list of sex toys for sex play, genius, I remind myself, is the ability to deviate — especially when you're desperate.

Some men, I read, enjoy having a woman cradle the penis with one hand while gently nibbling up the length of it, as if she were eating corn on the cob. Instead of corn, I try to picture myself nibbling on a row of freshly boiled Brussels sprouts.

Then there's "Tricks With Mints". You suck on an Altoid, a Halls cough drop, or just brush your teeth with Pepsodent. I have no mints, but Brussels sprouts I've got. I could stick two in each cheek . . . for a *different* sensation.

The author is big on pearls. In "His Pearl Necklace" she suggests licking his penis, then slowly adorning him with your pearls, gently wrapping the strand around his shaft. When his penis looks like it is wearing a Lady Diana choker, she writes, start stroking him, up and down, with a twist. Then unwrap his penis, as if you are flossing under his testicles, pulling it off.

Say what?

I am not cultured enough to wear pearls. I wonder if Brussels sprouts thawed and strung together would have the same effect?

On TV everyone who is still alive is eating dinner like it's their last meal, when a guy runs out of the kitchen with a jar of gherkins. Inside the jar is a pickled human finger. The guy throws it on the table and says, "What the hell is this?"

"That's Mikey's finger," says the host, chewing casually. "He used to be my bartender, 'til I caught him with his fingers in the till. When I open a new joint I put this jar in a very prominent place where everyone can see it. I put a very prominent label on the jar that says, 'This is Mikey's finger. It's here because he stole from his boss.' You steal once, you lose a finger. I catch you twice, you lose a hand. So far I only got a couple of hands. They're downstairs, in the freezer."

I reach across Stephen's body for *What Would Buddha Do? 101 Answers to Life's Daily Dilemmas*.

What would Buddha do to allow himself sexual pleasure? For starters, he suggests chanting "*Namu-myoho-renge-kyo*" during love-making, when the passions are first awakening. That, and a fistful of ice-cubes "at the right moment" and I'd have my man eating out of my palm.

"What's on the menu?" Stephen asks. Buddha is big on food, too, though he likes to keep it simple. "What would Buddha Do When Making a Salad?" suggests starting with a single leaf. But that's easier said than done when two seventeen-foot-high fences topped with razor-wire stand between you and anything smacking of nature. What would Buddha do if all he had was two pounds of frozen Brussels sprouts? He would probably say recite a mantra. Radiate loving-kindness. Remember your breathing.

Fuhgedaboudit. As Bertold Brecht said, "First grub, then ethics." I put that book aside and choose something, I hope, less ethical: *I Don't Bow to Buddhas*, the selected poems of Yuen Mei, a Chinese poet, a gourmet, and a "food writer", who died 200 years ago.

> Getting or losing: how to tell which is which?
> The spider so pleased with his artful web . . .
> not a single bug to eat.

"What's for dinner?" Stephen asks, a little more desperate this time. The last gangster's on his meat-hook in the freezer, meaning the movie is done.

What would Buddha do? Be in the moment, he would say. Start now. If I can distract my partner for long enough, dinner can wait until morning. Meanwhile I don't plan to starve. A mouthful of semen contains only six calories but enough Vitamin C, Vitamin B12, fructose, sulfur, zinc, copper, magnesium, potassium, calcium and a whole lot of other wholesome substances so that I won't even miss my One-A-Day Multiple Vitamin.

The next morning I discover some muscles that haven't been getting a work-out at Lady Fitness. I can open my eyes but my jaw aches so hard I can't pry open my mouth wide enough to stuff in the Potato Stuffed Blackened Chicken Stephen has over-baked for breakfast. I go back to bed, taking the bag of frozen Brussels sprouts for a compress.

THE ONLY BEAUTIFUL PRISON IN THE WORLD

William Head Federal Penitentiary, on a windswept rocky peninsula that juts out from the southern tip of Vancouver Island, doesn't *feel* like a prison, if a Siberian gulag scenario where men with shaved heads eat fish-eyeball soup, freeze to death in cells smaller than rich people's coffins, and receive no communication from the outside world is what you expect. Unfortunately, there is still a segment of our population who think that's the kind of "rehabilitation" prisoners should receive.

How quickly that attitude changes when someone you love — a son, husband, a father, a brother — breaks the law and gets locked up. Now you have become a prison visitor. What kind of treatment can you expect to receive?

Today we're lined up under the razor wire: the mothers and fathers and wives, lovers, children, cousins, a grandmother in a wheelchair — citizens from every different walk of life and socioeconomic position — waiting to be admitted to prison for the Easter Social. I remember another Easter fifteen years ago, same prison, when my daughter was four and wore her new pink frock and Easter bonnet. She and all the other wildlings were lined up in a field and then, *on your mark, get set, GO!* turned loose to search for candy eggs. My daughter, who liked to take her time inspecting the daffodils and tulips (which is where, at home, the Easter Bunny hid his tiny coloured eggs so the wood bugs wouldn't eat them) was left standing, empty basket in hand, while the kids who had done this in previous years, trampled the flowers, and each other, to get the most loot. A kindly guard must have felt sorry for my daughter, because she came hopping back to where we sat with a headless chocolate rabbit melting in her hands.

Today I sign in, strip off my jewelry, and walk through the metal detector. One of the female officers says she can smell alcohol. The guard checking my shoes ("one man got on a plane not long ago with explosives in his heels," he says, explaining his rationale) straightens up and moves closer to my face, as if he expects me now to open my mouth and breathe on him, which manners would not permit. The female officer sniffs the air again, then nods in the direction of the room where more security guards sit, behind an iron grill. "Someone drinking on the job?" she asks the guard who examined my shoes. The visitors look at one another, relieved. If it had been one of us, we would have been told to leave the prison, and there would have been consequences.

But a guard with a substance abuse problem? I try not to disapprove. After all, my husband and ninety percent of the other men inside these walls are here because of an addiction — in most cases, addictions that get out of hand. I find myself hoping the guard can do something about his drinking problem before he loses his job and gets desperate enough to rob a bank.

A prison Social is like an Open House: anyone on a prisoner's list can visit. Sometimes there are bands playing music, the kids can knock a baseball around and get a free hot dog from the CON CESSION. Today the gymnasium is decorated with pastel-coloured balloons, for Easter.

My husband has set up a table outside, in a little grotto: he's made a simple fruit salad and cookies for his guests. In the middle of the table is a teapot, a box of Gunpowder tea, and a basket of foil-wrapped chocolate Easter eggs for our daughter, who, at the last minute, decided not to come today.

I sit in the sun holding my husband's hand, watching the wind in the trees, the distant mountains, the hammered-pewter surface of the sea. This place of terrible beauty was a quarantine station before it became another kind of prison. My husband's favourite spot is the graveyard on the southern side, which we can see from where we sit — the final resting place of those travellers who never quite made the last leg of their journey to the New World. Their graves are marked with a date, their name, and the name of the ship they sailed in on, like the grave my husband often goes to sit beside: Liza Gentel, 1901-1911, Empress of Russia. Our own daughter's age.

Other convicts and their families stop by to pay their respects, as is the custom. Lama Margaret, the Buddhist nun who comes here to visit the men who have no one, tells me they have banned prisoners from the Meditation Garden because, they say, it's a security risk. I think how much is taken from us these days in the name of enhanced security.

A young Chinese prisoner comes to sit with us. He calls my husband "Ah-kung", Grandfather. He says we will do business together when he gets out in six months time and returns to Canton. "No monkey business," my husband says, laughing. I say he must be glad not to be in prison in China where I have read men are executed for writing bad cheques, and the family is sent the bullet casing afterwards, and expected to pay for it. He nods and smiles, nods and smiles.

Everywhere I look I see children. Fathers tossing children in the air, wrestling with them, jogging with them on their shoulders. Big men with big tattoos cradling newborn babies on their knees. Old grandfather-convicts with faraway eyes photographed with their gang of grandchildren. In America, 1.5 million children have parents in prison. I wonder what the statistics are here.

Our friends don't arrive, which is out of character. I stay until dark clouds cover the sun and all the cookies are gone. There's a note on my car from our friends who had been turned away at the gate: Brian's ferry from Salt Spring was late because of spring break and increased traffic. I talk to him on the phone later in the evening; he says the guard had come on the loudspeaker and said, curtly, "You're too late." Brian looked at his watch, which said 2:02. "Gates close at 2:00," the guard said. "That's it."

I try to be understanding. I remind myself: we don't get guards from Planet Compassionate. We get them from Earth. Still, it hurts . . . when you're a friend of a family member and you get treated as part of the problem, not part of the cure.

William Head Penitentiary may be beautiful from the outside, but as all prisoners, their families and their visitors, and the guards who do their own kind of time here, know: the only beautiful prison in the world is the one you leave behind.

ORGY IN THE INTERFAITH CHAPEL

At the advice of my doctor who felt I might have become "a touch paranoid" when I told him "there are more of them than there are of us," I made an appointment with a psychiatrist. Once a week I spend an hour telling him about my dysfunctional relationship with a machine.

The Itemizer machine, the alleged state-of-the-art successor to the dreaded ion-scanner, is a by-product of yet another American-made loser of a war (the age-old one, on drugs) purportedly able to detect microscopic particles of illicit substances. Corrections Services Canada has foisted this machine on our country's penitentiaries, at a cost of $60,000 a hit. The problem is, the Itemizer can't always tell the difference between hand lotion and LSD.

When the machine first reared its capricious head at William Head Institution in August 2002, numbers of visitors, all known non-drug users, began testing false-positive for everything from marijuana to heroin, and several octogenarian church-goers for crystal meth. Not everyone who attends is a saint, but even a skeptic would be hard-pressed to picture Sunday afternoon in the prison's Interfaith Chapel as an orgy of methamphetamine abuse.

I took precautions. Before visiting my husband I bathed, donned freshly laundered clothes, and scoured my hands, my watch, and wedding band with a vegetable brush. The Itemizer gave me the thumb's up every time, until the day I let my guard down and applied a Body Shop Soy Butter Cream to my skin after my bath. An hour later, at the prison's front gate, the Itemizer's alarm sounded, Red Alert! My watch had tested positive for cocaine.

When a visitor tests "positive" she is informed that, while no one accuses her of smuggling drugs into the joint, her visit is being denied because she is deemed to have come into contact with drugs. Wild amounts of drugs. Corrections stands behind the American manufacturers who maintain the Itemizer has been calibrated so as not to register "casual contact" (contact with the sixty percent of paper money which, according to the Bank of Canada, contains cocaine residue), that in order to test positive I must first have shaken hands with the Medellin cartel.

I seriously doubt whether the Body Shop buffs up their Soy Butter Cream with cocaine to make it go further, but this was the only explanation I was able to offer the prison's Visits Review Board, before whom I appeared a week later. (Another visitor's hand cream had tested positive for heroin, I learned.) The Board thought bleach might be the best cleaning product to use ("Try Clorox Wipes," one member suggested) if I was concerned about possible contamination from prison door knobs, etc. Even paranoids have enemies, after all. Why not microscopic ones?

On my next visit my bracelet, made from 22-calibre bullet shells (if I'm guilty of anything it's the delight I take in watching bullets being scanned for microscopic particles of drugs) which I had cleaned with a Clorox Wipe, tested positive — for LSD. Several days later, the prison chaplain, who'd heard of my nightmare, offered his watch for inspection — it tested negative. He cleaned it with a Clorox Wipe and asked to have it scanned again: this time it tested positive — not for LSD, but for cocaine.

The machine was given a time out, until a snake oil salesman blew in from the US to recalibrate it so that it no longer confused Clorox Wipes with a controlled substance. But what about the thousands of other innocent cleaning products, perfumes, toiletries, prescription drugs, that have the same molecular responses as the active ingredients in narcotics? How many more visitors to prison must suffer unnecessary humiliation in the hands of a machine that has proven itself utterly capable of making inhuman errors?

Corrections claims that family is the single most important rehabilitative tool in a prisoner's reformation. One woman, First Nations, who appeared before the Visits Review Board with a native elder who was recovering from a hip operation when she had tested false-positive for Ecstasy, told me she will no longer bring her children to see their father; she blames the Itemizer for breaking families apart. (A forty-six-year-old inmate hanged himself last fall after his eighty-two-year-old mother tested false-positive for cocaine and was turned away at the front gate. She never saw her son again.)

The Itemizer machine should be sent packing from our prisons until it can be programmed to tell the difference between right and wrong. I would sooner submit to random urinalysis or a full body search, including vaginal and rectal, if that is what it takes to ensure my visits are not interfered with. Any invasive procedure would seem far less inhumane and demeaning than the situation prison visitors must endure.

FIFTEEN YEARS

I slip off my wedding ring, which doesn't fit so snugly anymore, and add it to the plastic tray along with my two silver bracelets. Then I step through the metal detector. On my wedding day, fifteen years ago today, my French garters lit up the alert panel to the highest number, ten.

I married Stephen in a maximum security prison. He had written a novel while finishing off a twenty-year sentence for gold robbery, and the manuscript had landed on my desk when I was Writer-in-Residence at the University of Waterloo in Ontario. I fell in love: with his writing on the first page, and with him before first sight.

I visited him behind bars for two years before asking him to marry me. There was a small problem — I was already married at the time — but nothing our love couldn't rise above.

After leaving the prison chapel, tossing my bouquet over the fourteen-foot-high perimeter fence topped with razor-wire, and watching it land on the butt of a prison guard's M-16 rifle, there was the honeymoon — a three-day affair in a cottage inside the prison walls allocated for Private Family Visits. A conjugal visit, in the vernacular, but that makes it sound as if it's only about sex. Nine months later, our daughter was born, Stephen's novel was published, and he came home on full parole. We lived together not, unhappily, for ever after.

Our married life went into remission the day my husband failed to successfully rob the Royal Bank in the peaceful Cook Street Village, in Victoria, British Columbia on June 9th, 1999. Stephen remembers little of the car chase through Beacon Hill Park, or shooting at police officers who pursued him.

A guard pulls on a pair of black gloves and goes through our personal effects, most of which I have itemized. My daughter, who is twelve, has brought her French homework and a suitcase whose contents I *haven't* bothered to list. The guard opens the bag, and shuts it again, immediately. She must have a daughter who wears make-up, too.

My belongings are more problematic. She vetoes my vitamins, and my pillow, citing enhanced security. My pillow and I are bonded like Brinks guards; ever since I was four years old and my mother threw my stuffed rabbit in the fire (they didn't have child psychology back then) because I kept losing it in the night, my pillow has represented security. I never leave home without it

Now I have a choice to make — my security or my marriage. I stuff the pillow and my vitamins in a locker marked Private Family Visits, which smells of sweaty shoes and cigarette smoke, reminding myself marriage involves sacrifice. Stephen shaking it rough for eighteen years is small beer compared to the three nights looming ahead of me without my pillow, but I vow not to make an issue over it. I start planning instead. A false-bottomed suitcase would be one solution.

If my pillow posed a security threat I have a feeling that what the guard comes upon next will make headlines in the *National Enquirer*: "Female Counterpart to Osama bin Laden Allowed Conjugal Visit". I spent all morning polishing the Georgian silver flatware she calls "utensils".

I never use stainless — "it leaves a taste," as my father always said — and just because I am going to prison I don't see why I should be expected to lower my standards. The knives are bone-handled, passed down from William the Conqueror. And our table-napkin rings, with family crest and initials engraved: oh, what's the use, I think, and into the vile-smelling locker go my valuables — along with my values and my standards — all of little consequence, I suppose, where security is at stake.

Now she inspects my briefcase, full of books and magazines. When she questions why I have brought so many I tell her I need different books for different moods, and who can predict what mood I'll be in by this evening, given I'll be . . . the words "without my pillow" hang unspoken between us.

She turns her attention to my magazines. I've brought a new *Martha Stewart Living* (I was trying to be a good citizen and supported my daughter's school magazine drive) and two back issues of *Colors*: one devoted to War, the other to Touch. She would have to open the latter, on whose cover two naked men of different ethnic persuasions are vigorously French-kissing.

Colors, I explain, as I see her frowning as she flips through the pages, is an art magazine. "Doesn't look therapeutic to me," she says, letting me know she thinks art, and Private Family Visits, are viewed as therapy. She puts the magazine down and opens the *Martha Stewart Living*. My daughter says to her, "That's the *really* subversive one."

When we're repacked, we're told to stand side-by-side on two yellow dots in the middle of the floor. A black dog, trained to sniff out drugs, is led into the room. I pray my daughter, who is at that age, has not decided to bring the pot she grew for a school Science project to impress her Dad. It turns out I have nothing to worry about. The dog doesn't sit (as he's trained to do when he scores). When I try to explain to my daughter why we are being searched — because some people have been known to smuggle drugs into the institution — she says, "Don't they know anything? People come to prison to *buy* their weed. They get the best bud in here."

She's twelve years old. How can she know this? In the Private Family Visiting cottage she curls up with *Colors* — the Touch issue — while my husband and I unpack the supplies he's bought for our three days of conjugal bliss.

Of course he has the good stuff stashed away: the zuzus and wham whams he and my daughter like to eat while they watch mindless TV. "Mum, this is like totally sick," our daughter says, tossing aside the magazine she's been engrossed in. "No wonder they didn't want you showing it to Dad."

Her dad and I grab it to see what we have been missing. If a twelve-year-old thinks it's sick, it has to be.

We open to a man wearing black socks — you can't see his face because his head is in a pillory — and black underpants pulled naughtily down. A busty leather-clad dominatrix is lashing his red bottom with a whip. "When it starts to get intense," she says, "they wriggle and squirm, they use swear words occasionally but they stay in place." I want to rush back to the front gate and explain to the guard, this is *art*, not pornography, and besides, I didn't know this photograph was there. "What *are* they going to think of me?" I cry. "They'll think I'm some kind of pervert."

"They'll just think *I* perverted you," my husband sighs. "They think all inmates are criminals."

For the next three days and nights we will live like a normal family, though nothing seems normal to me without my pillow. At the risk of being called a martyr, I decide it's important to make my husband aware of how much I have sacrificed to spend this quality time with him. When he stops laughing he reminds me that I have crossed international borders with everything from an inflatable alligator (when I was nine) to emeralds (much later) concealed on my body. Now I am considering having a special suitcase made for my — pillow?

I'm sorry I mentioned it, I say. Conjugal bliss is beginning to feel an awful lot like marriage.

In most respects, though, I could adapt to prison life quite easily. We have a panoramic view of the majestic razor-wire surrounding our abode, and the phone only rings four times a day, and it's never for me. When it does ring, though, we must get up, go outside, and be counted. Sometimes they call back right away and we have to go out again for a recount. How hard can it be, my daughter asks her dad, to count to three?

We cook, read, play Scrabble on the floor, watch movies — about drug trafficking and prison escapes, which, judging by how many there are, the public must find therapeutic. In a drawer beside our bed I discover a Tupperware container full of condoms, lubricants, latex gloves, and dams, like the ones the dentist puts in your mouth (for safe oral sex I suppose), and a miniature bottle of bleach — for those who *do* manage to smuggle in their hypodermic needles. It's a weird system: *we'll bust your ass if we catch you bringing in drugs, but if you succeed, use clean needles.* We conjugate, too. French verbs. For my daughter's French test on Monday.

October 12th, the day of our wedding anniversary (I remembered it as being the 10th, Stephen the 15th; I checked when I got home and we were both wrong), we pack again and prepare to say our goodbyes. But first we clean the cottage, washing the floors, vacuuming the rugs and then raking them so that our footprints don't show. My husband has learned many new domestic skills since coming back to jail. These days he says he exchanges muffin recipes instead of tunnel plans out in the big yard.

It's check-out time and we have our bags ready when the van arrives to deliver us back to the prison's front gate. But another van pulls up behind it and now we're ordered back inside and told to line up in the living room, side-by-side, on the very spot where I made the word INNOCENT at Scrabble last night and scored fifteen points.

The same dog we met on the way into our visit is led into the middle of my husband's newly raked carpet. He walks around us — not once, but four times; he noses our crotches and our behinds, leaving his drool. It's humiliating. It's unnecessary. It's intimidation, I guess.

Then I think, maybe my daughter is right. Maybe people do come here to buy the good drugs. It's evident that we're suspected of trying to smuggle *something* out of this place, and it clearly isn't my husband, who is staring at his feet. I will never know what it feels like to be a man and watch, powerlessly, as your family is (in his eyes, anyway) violated.

If I had tears left, I would weep, but instead I stand, shaken, angry (for a target search such as this they have to be ninety-nine percent certain they'll find drugs), and, I admit, tired of it. (My daughter tells me later, when the dog doesn't sit and we're free to go, she thinks the warden saw the bumper sticker on my car saying BAD COP, NO DOUGHNUT, and was getting revenge.)

One reason I've stayed married to the same man for fifteen years is that he always surprises me; I never know what he's going to do next. The usual anniversary present for couples celebrating fifteen years of marriage is crystal, but trust Stephen to come up with something more romantic. At least *I* think it's romantic to get drooled on by a drug dog for your fifteenth wedding anniversary. Definitely the kind of love I want. And, lest I forget (writing being the best revenge), I got material, too.

A GRIEF OBSERVED

The Posthumous

ROBIN SKELTON, 1925 – 1977

"The wind's in the west tonight,/ heavy with tidal sound," begins his "Night Poem, Vancouver Island". The West Coast's literary Magus, wizard of the measured line, wearer of big hats and big whiskers, editor, translator, biographer, short-story writer, inventor of the erotic surrealist Georges Zuk, stamp collector, former Chair of the Writers' Union, artist, and scholar, died on August 22nd, aged seventy-one, at his home in Victoria. A bibliophile who had over 30,000 books in his library, magician, witch, healer — he put more cancer in remission, banished more warts, and blessed more houses than anyone I've known — he devoted his life, first and foremost, to poetry, to the Muse, and to Sylvia, his wife of forty years, his Muse incarnate.

Robin Skelton, born in East Yorkshire on October 25th, 1925, was an only child who read Chaucer before he was seven and composed his first poem when he was eight-and-a-half years old. "The sails were set/ The sailors got wet." ("Well, at least it rhymed," he said.) He emigrated to Canada in 1963 and became an associate professor in the English Department at the University of Victoria; four years later he founded *The Malahat Review*, an international journal of arts and letters, and planned a comprehensive Creative Writing program, of which he became the Founding Chair in 1973. His reputation was legendary; he was teacher, mentor, and an inspiration to many who went on to lead lives "created by poetry".

I had just celebrated my sixteenth birthday — locked in Room 0 of the psychiatric wing at a Victoria hospital — when Robin came to visit me; he had met my psychiatrist at a drinks party. Previously, I had babysat his three young children, Nicholas, Alison, and Brigid, but we had spoken only casually. I remember being in awe of his house because there was *art*, modern art on the walls, and books everywhere. At least thirty of the books were ones Robin himself had written. I remember touching them, as if some of their magic might rub off. I had just begun to write poetry myself.

At the hospital, over a cup of tea because there wasn't anything stronger, Robin asked to see some of my work. After reading a handful of my poems, he told me, "You're not mad, you're a poet." He published six of those early poems in *The Malahat Review*, and with my $100 earnings I bought my first typewriter. Subsequently, he insisted that he had simply pointed me in the direction my life was meant to be taking. "Poetry creates the poet, and not vice versa," he said.

In his *Memoirs of a Literary Blockhead* this remarkable man of Letters describes himself, somewhat self-effacingly for one who has published more than a hundred books, as a "minor Pooh-Bah" with a peculiar talent for "confusing confusion". It is true he never learned to drive a car, and had to be reminded to look both ways before crossing the street, but he was also extremely capable, and always *there* when you needed him. He was the person I would call when I needed to know a point of grammar, or settle an argument: was Irish whiskey made from barley or rye or potato peelings — or — what exactly? He could drink more Jameson's than any person I know, and not get drunk. He had a great wit, an easy charm; he was able to laugh at himself and the comical turns he saw his own life sometimes taking.

In 1983, on a reading tour of Ireland, accompanied by my husband and small daughter, I got to know him even more intimately. He ate the Mixed Grill every night for dinner (bacon, eggs, sausage, chips, peas, and black pudding all fried in yesterday's bacon grease) and the same for breakfast (fried in last night's grease). He announced, halfway through the tour, that he would be taking his bi-monthly bath. In the interest of saving more water, presumably, he hung his socks out the window to air as we criss-crossed the country, giving nineteen poetry readings in twenty-one days. In Limerick, when we were offered "a presbyterian" (non-alcoholic beverage, in this case a cup of tea), Robin asked if they had anything stronger. "Mineral water?" asked our host. It was the only time I ever saw Robin speechless.

What else do I remember? The way he called you "luv" with a Yorkshire accent; that he was the only person alive I allowed to call me Sue, the only person I've known with enough nerve to send back a bottle of Yago Blanco for being "off" (I'd always assumed that was the way it tasted). That he and Sylvia reorganized their house and altered their lives over and over again to make room for their aged parents so they wouldn't have to go to a nursing home. That their house, over the years, welcomed numerous young people who were in one kind of trouble or another, and who needed a place of refuge. That the death of his son, Nicholas, in 1994, left a hole in his heart, and that the subsequent death of his friend, the poet Charles Lillard, made the hole so much bigger his heart could no longer close around it and go on beating. That he was loyal. That he hated talking on the telephone as much as I do, which is why we both waited for the other one to call first, and why I didn't get to say goodbye. That when he laughed it sounded like a fistful of mice being forced through a tortilla press. That his very presence blessed us.

In *Skelton at 60*, a symposium published to celebrate and honour Robin on his sixtieth birthday, Margaret Atwood penned "Floreat Skeltonus", which ends "His giggle is much like the hiss of a kettle/ Watch out though, his mind's like a trap made of metal./ But is he a Druid disguised as a bear,/ Or a bear as a Druid? One has to declare/ It's anyone's guess. The main thing is, he's *there*."

He was, and always will be. And because I believe the poet should have the last word, always, here are the last lines of the final stanza of "Night Poem, Vancouver Island", a poem that has imprinted his timeless voice on our literary and intellectual landscape:

Light rises from the sea
and time spreads with the light.
Put your body to mine;
we are the world we caused.

WILLIAM MARTIN HOFFER, 1944 – 1997

In early September, I sat with Bill Hoffer in his parent's windy garden in Victoria where a patio door kept banging open and almost shut. "I've always thought life had something to do with the speed at which one walked through certain museums," he told me, approaching the subject of his mortality as he did every subject — any way but overtly. "In some cases if you walked too slowly you would become part of the permanent exhibits."

William Martin Hoffer, antiquarian bookseller, publisher, man of letters, friend to many writers, and, he would want me to say, enemy to others, became part of the permanent on September 28, 1997, stubbed out by lung cancer ("I've had to give up cigarettes for the time-being") in his fifty-third year. Peter Howard, of Serendipity Books in Berkeley, who is contributing to a memorial volume for Bill's family, speaks for many of us: "He had burned very brightly. No filter. He was my friend. I tried to be his."

Born in Winnipeg on May 29th, 1944, Bill attended the University of Saskatchewan and Simon Fraser University where he agitated, politically. "I hide in the house and blacken the windows whenever a peace march goes by," he once told me. He married in 1965 and agitated, personally; he intended a first volume of poetry to be *The Plague Years*. He revered his father, Dr. Abram Hoffer, co-founder of orthomolecular medicine, who, in his eyes, "deserved the Nobel Prize;" when his mother co-authored *Everybody's Favourite Orthomolecular Muffin Recipes*, he seemed shyly pleased. He suffered from depression and diabetes; insulin reactions put him, more than a few times, in the hospital. Even on the many occasions when he tried to quit smoking, he always nursed an unlit cigarette.

I met Bill in his shop — Falstaff Books on 10th Avenue in Vancouver, formerly an abortion clinic — in 1970. Somewhere between explaining to me why there was a dash after my birth year (1951–) on the copyright page of my book, and the moment I spooned bookbinder's glue into my tea, thinking it was honey, Bill became my literary executor.

After 10th Avenue he moved to Granville Street, on the second floor directly above The Love Shop, which sold sexual paraphernalia. He published eighty catalogues (he called them "lists") that increasingly included hostile remarks about most Canadian writers, publishers, and government subsidies to the arts. Towards the end he denounced many Canadian writers as "war criminals," declared Canadian literature contaminate, named his campaign TANKS ARE MIGHTY FINE THINGS, and promised to burn his entire stock of blewointment press publications in a black-tie event in his parking lot — one promise he failed to keep.

His last bookstore-bastion was on Powell Street, in Gastown, (now a transsexual hair salon), its windows grated, doors barred, and double-locked. Here Bill slept, cooked, entertained, strummed a 1957 Dreadnaught guitar (as if with a belt buckle, one potential customer gloomily observed), and held curmudgeonly court behind his desk, deciding whether or not to let a potential customer come inside. If he didn't like the look of you once you *were* inside, he wouldn't sell you a book. "At least there won't be any obituaries," he told me, shortly before his last trip to the hospital.

His friends, though, saw his compassionate side (he was patient with me when I put bookglue in my tea) and the great pains he took to make sure most people didn't notice.

In the early 1990s he began to study Russian. He enrolled in a summer school for foreigners in Moscow where he met and married a young widow with two teenaged children. He amassed the biggest private collection of handmade wooden and clay toys — over 3000 of them — in the country. He read Dostoevsky in Russian. He listened to Mozart's *Requiem*. After being diagnosed with cancer in Moscow, he put himself in his father's care, travelling 8000 miles home to do so.

He arrived too late. In the Jubilee Hospital a nurse came to check his vital signs. "And what was it like living in Moscow?" she asked, distracting him from worrying about the pulse she couldn't find.

"It wasn't Gabereau. It wasn't *Saturday Night*. It wasn't the hideous assassination of Margaret Laurence — I knew they'd turn on her in the end because she drank."

Bill, in fighting form, to the very end. The nurse, I think, suspected it was dementia. She didn't know Bill.

He was intense, articulate, funny, profound. I have notebooks filled with the memorable words he's given to me. In the hospital, the night before he died, he said, "I've always said such stupid things to you." And in that final room, with a few bone-coloured carnations in a jar beside his bed, I held his magnificent hands and said something equally stupid back.

Peter Howard sent his memoir to Bill's wife in Moscow. "When I saw on the computer's screen these two dates with a dash between then, 1944 – 1997, I felt like I was hit on my head with the unhappiness of all people on Earth," Masha wrote, of her *Bilochka*.

That early fall day, in his parent's windy garden, Bill said, "Please don't be unhappy about me." And the door banged shut.

AL PURDY, 1918 – 2000

I met Al Purdy in Mexico — in the Yucatan — in 1972. He and his wife, Eurithe, were travelling on poet's wages — staying in cheap motels, shopping for meat and potatoes in the markets, and cooking on their own hot-plate. They must have blown up every electrical circuit in the Yucatan. I was all of twenty at the time; I'd never met anyone like Al, and though he was one of the most difficult men, in my young, nervous way, I grew to love him. (How could anyone resist a poet who takes his own hot-plate to Mexico?) Al was larger-than-life-size in every way. When he grabbed you by the arm to talk seriously about the thing he loved best — poetry — he always left a mark.

I knew his poetry. I knew no subject was too small or too awkward for Purdy, with his meat and potatoes, small-town Canadian sensibility as big as the world's. His poems had a way of exuding what Seamus Heaney has called, "some of the smelly majesty of living."

I also knew the myth, through the poetry others had written about him, my favourite being "Purdy's Crocuses" by Tom Wayman. Purdy went to work as Writer-in-Residence at Loyola in Montreal with a twelve-pack of beer under each arm, and twice a week would sit talking to students, reading their poems, and drinking. He'd recycle his bottles by tossing them out the window.

In the spring, the first thing that appeared out of the melting snow under his office window was a beer bottle — one, then another, until the whole term's pile of empties was uncovered: Purdy's crocuses, the students called them. Wayman writes that now whenever he drives across the country (a journey Al and Eurithe made several times each year, from Ameliasburgh to the West Coast) he doesn't mind so much seeing the dozens of empty beer bottles along the edges of northern Ontario's lonely hardtop, or on Saskatchewan's soft verges.

What the poet planted in Montreal
has taken hold, spread coast-to-coast . . .
slowly the shoulders of the main highways, and the ditches
along every back road in Canada
are filling with the brown blooms of Purdy's crocuses.

At one time in his life, Purdy would have been pleased to have the image of a beer bottle evoke his memory. Those were the days when he was known as the hard-drinking, bar-brawling-but-sensitive man; I only really got to know him after he'd stopped drinking, and started listening (a little). And he wasn't easy, as they say in Ireland. Al could never be easy.

For one thing, he would never let you get away with a word used casually or without forethought. If you said hello he would ask if you really meant it. Once, when he came to read his poetry at the University of Waterloo where I was Writer-in-Residence, a few of us took him to lunch at the Faculty Club. Al began by picking the tiny shreds of grated carrot out of his salad. "Carrots," he said, with a certain amount of horror, as if he had encountered two slugs mating in his radicchio. And, with even more of a sneer, "Health food."

When the waiter returned and asked if Al would care for a bun, I knew the poor boy was in for it. "Yes," Al said, after considering the matter deeply and for a long time. "I *would* care for a bun. I care for my wife, too. I care for many things. What about you? What do you care for?"

The waiter put the bun on the poet's side plate, but with excessive hesitation. Purdy was a man who took words as they were meant to be taken — seriously — and from that moment on, whenever I was in his company, I tripped over everything I had to say, and Purdy took big pleasure in tripping me up every time.

~ ~ ~

Wherever I have travelled, Al Purdy has been there first. And written poems about it. For instance, when I reached an age where I began to have a love affair with Paris, along came Purdy with *To Paris Never Again*. Purdy doesn't romance the City the way I did last spring, drinking the best wine in a new good restaurant every night, leaving baby's breath on Oscar Wilde's grave in Pere LaChaisse, taking a boat trip down the Seine in the rain, being followed through the narrow streets by a gypsy fire breather who said he could make the rain stop falling. Purdy, his stomach upset from the drinking water, finds a flea-infested room near the Metro where the noise of the train shakes him awake all night, sucking him out of bed as he dreams of Marie Antoinette and Eleanor of Aquitaine "in a castle the size of Alberta." One of the things I loved about Al is that he could travel the world and write poems that never stop reminding us of his — and our own — Canadianness. Perhaps he was the quintessential Canadian: a foreigner wherever he went, and always being mistaken for an American.

His words often take us "somewhere close to happiness"and for holidays in the secret places his poetry lets us discover inside ourselves. He takes us with him when he travels back through the centuries into a marble bath with Agamemnon, King of Mycenae, as he washes off the dust of travel on his return from Troy, or climbs a mountain road in Mexico in low gear, or flies across the prairies where "9/10ths of the landscape is sky/ more sunlit heaven than earth," or stands outside naked in the snow, "in the lazy plunge and swirl of falling things."

There are few places anyone can go on this planet, in fact, that Purdy has not been, and written about, whether it be in the Peruvian Andes, at Machu Pichu, where he's rejoicing that he's alive in those mountains — "that life should bring such gifts/ and wrap them in clouds and stars," or at an extended care facility in Quesnel, interviewing an ancient woman for his BC ghost towns article, or lost in a telephone booth trying to phone God. Even his poems for the dead speak of journeys, how he is unable to join his dead friends in that "unknown country" but how he has "invented imaginary souls for them/ that kept on living when they died."

"And what am I but what I remember" he asks, in "The Names the Names" (so many dead friends, their names gone into the dark). Friends like Tom:

years ago when he was especially boring
and I was taking pride in my bad manners
I told him so and he said
"I hope that won't make any difference
to our friendship"
which till then I hadn't known existed
but after that it did . . .

～～～

Our own friendship blossomed (though blossoming is not a word one immediately associates with Al) in 1988 when the Purdys bought a house on the outskirts of Sidney on Vancouver Island. It became clear that my new neighbour would not easily adjust from rural Prince Edward County to living across the road from what I, as a child growing up in the area, had dubbed "the Cold and Windy Beach". I don't remember how it happened, but their house became infested with fleas. Al, his legs covered with red, itchy bites took to dressing in three pairs of wool work socks up to his knees, with his trousers — the kind he had to buy at the Extra Big and Tall Second Hand shop — tucked in at the top. When the fleas moved into the wool, he prepared to repair to Ameliasburgh, and leave the West Coast to the bug life and other, less sensitive poets.

Marilyn Bowering came up with a solution for him at a party. She said a raccoon rids himself of fleas by taking a piece of grass in his teeth, swimming out into the middle of a lake, then ducking under water with only the tip of the grass sticking out. The fleas would stampede onto the grass, the raccoon would let go of it, and swim back, unencumbered, to shore.

I still have an image of Al, crossing the road to the Cold and Windy Beach, one of his well-masticated wooden matches hanging from the corner of his mouth, power-walking into the cold Pacific. This may be the only time I ever saw him exercise. Al was not big on either health food or being physically fit. His world was of the mind, and there he never lost his grip. Never loosened it for an instant. A week before he died I was sitting at the end of his bed, which felt unusually warm. When I realized I was sitting on his heating pad, I said, "Ohhhhhhhh! I wondered why the bed was so hot!"

"Can't be all that hot, my ass is further up," he gasped, lifting himself so I could see the view.

"Yes," I said, "I see."

"You see?" Al said, making as if to further loosen his dressing gown.

"In a manner of speaking," I said. Even as he lay dying, he wouldn't let me off the hook.

∽ ∽ ∽

Though our longest sun sets at right declensions and makes
but winter arches, it cannot be long before we lie down
in darkness
and have our light in ashes . . .

— Browne: *Urn Burial*

In April, the cruelest month of 1999, when Al Purdy was diagnosed as having a tumour on his lung, he didn't refuse to talk about it. Al looked at death the same way he has always looked at life — right between the eyes. ("Nothing is permanent. Our eternal shortness of existence ensures it," he once wrote to me.) When he told me the news he also offered me his last two unopened packages of typing paper, which seemed like a tragically final gesture but also a tragically generous gesture for one who picked up free day-old bread at the Salvation Army and confessed to using bleach to remove the postage marks on stamps. Of the paper, he said, "I won't be needing it." (When I insisted he might still have reams to write before he slept, Eurithe took one of the packages back, but I kept the other.)

All of us, his friends, tried to be brave. Some dedicated poems to him, some sent flowers. Patrick Lane obsessively baked bread — more than Al could eat in a lifetime. "Why don't you hurry up and die so I can stop baking!" Patrick demanded, at the last dinner party where the six of us were together. My husband cut wood on Al and Eurithe's beach during the storms that last spring, to keep our home fires burning.

Each time I visited their house, Al asked me if, when the time came, I would like some of his ashes. Each time, I squirmed, it being hard to imagine someone who takes up the enormous psychic and physical space Al does in the world, having his light in ashes.

Finally, I responded the only way I could, by writing a poem — "32 Uses for Al Purdy's Ashes" — that is more of a tribute to his poetry, than a poem about mortality. The poem begins:

Smuggle them to Paris and fling them
into the Seine. P.S. He was wrong
when he wrote, "To Paris Never Again"

and goes on to suggest various other ways of employing his mortal remains: putting them in an egg-timer so he could go on being useful; sprinkling them, when you're stuck in deep snow, under your bald tires for traction; declaring them culturally modified property and having them preserved for posterity in the Museum of Modern Man and, as Purdy would be the first to add, Modern Wife; placing them beside your bed where they can watch you make love, vulgarly and immensely, in the little time left.

Al seemed pleased with the poem, though he grew less enthused with it the closer he came to death. The day before he died (he died on Good Friday) he told me the best lines in my poem were his, and demanded fifty percent of any money I made, in perpetuity. He was right, of course. The best lines are always his. And, as always, he got there first.

> — and now far into old age
> with its inevitable conclusion
> I am deeply troubled
> a profound literary sadness
> of knowing I am using death
> too much in poems
> but turn about
> is fair play I guess and
> I expect to have it use me
> soon for its own purposes
> whatever those might be
> and it won't be for poems.

One day when I reach that "unknown country" myself, there is one thing I'll know: Al Purdy will have been there and written a poem about it, before moving on to wherever it is we go.

"SOFTLY I GO NOW, PAD PAD"
— Stevie Smith

Last fall I rescued (or so I believed at the time) a crazy tree-climbing cat from a life spent high in the windy branches of a hemlock on Haida Gwaii. (Bitz made her cameo appearance earlier in this book, in the essay "Writer, Interrupted".) I flew her south with me, to live on Vancouver Island. On Good Friday, in 2004, Bitz ran out onto West Saanich Road, smack into something you won't find in any treetop: a Honda Accord. The woman she'd hit stopped; I found her standing in my driveway, crying, "I'm a cat person, too."

Bitz made it as far as the gate, fell at my feet, and lay, staring up at me. I wrung my hands; I prayed *maybe she has just been stunned*, though the trickle of blood at the corner of her mouth was a small grief with a short life, and a death of its own. She died, twenty minutes later, in my daughter's arms, at the vet's.

Everything reminded me of her, from the can opener to the litter box, and went through me like a spear. In the garden I started digging a grave beside the last cat I loved who failed to look both ways — but then the lines of a poem, one by Robinson Jeffers, came flaring back: "To rot in the earth/ is a loathsome end, but to roar up in flames — besides I am used to it/ I have flamed with love and fury so often in my life . . . "

Bitz, who had spent her small lifetime reaching for the sky, would not have chosen the earth for a final resting place. I decided I'd have her cremated and take her home to Haida Gwaii where she could live again, in the wind, in the tree I spent most of last summer trying to entice her out of.

Over the next weeks I had to unload my grief on everyone I met. I remembered another poem, Lorna Crozier's: she has been crying for days over her cat and knows there are some humans she can share this with but others who will reply, "He's only a cat." She now divides people into these two camps. "It's one way of knowing the world."

She was "only a cat" and I had three others — older, wiser, more grounded (in all senses of the word) — to console me as I struggled to know the world again, any way I could. There were the people, too, who tried to comfort me with the familiar words we use when faced with someone else's loss.

"All things must pass."

"It was her time."

"The only earthly certainty is oblivion."

Few, I realized, could bring themselves to speak the word *dead*.

C.S. Lewis, in "A Grief Observed", wrote about how his faith, even in God, was shaken when his wife died of cancer. "I look up at the night sky: is anything more certain that in all those vast times and spaces, if I were allowed to search I should nowhere find her face, her voice, her touch. She died. She is dead. Is the word so difficult to learn?"

She will live forever in your memory. Something else the well-meaning repeat. But *live* is precisely what Bitz would not do — ever again. All I had left of her was in ashes, and my unappeasable grief.

I tried revisiting her favourite places — as if it would bring her back to me — but it didn't help. Whether it was up on the shed roof (sometimes I would "rescue" her three times a day) or where she napped between my feet, on my office floor, she had become, everywhere, lost to me. "Death is a scatterer," wrote Stevie Smith. "He scatters the human frame/ The nerviness and the great pain/ Throws it on the fresh fresh air/ And now it is nowhere."

When someone we love dies, we are told, "She is happy now, at peace, in God's hands." Wasn't Bitz in God's hands when she bolted onto the road? Or do His hands hold onto us more fiercely the moment we leave our body and fly off? And if so, why?

I have no good pictures of Bitz — she never stood still long enough when being photographed — and now two months later, already I can't remember her body in any detail. And yet it is her body, her particularity — the way she let me pluck her off the shed roof, the way she clung to me, all grateful, purring warmth, as we descended the ladder — I miss.

C.S. Lewis says passionate grief does not link us to the dead, but cuts us off from them. Grief makes the dead far *more* dead. Paradoxically, when we let go, the less we mourn, the closer to our lost one we will get.

And he gives good reasons for grief. "It comes from the frustration of so many impulses that have become habitual. Thought after thought, feeling after feeling, action after action have our loved one for their object. Now their target is gone. We keep on through habit fitting an arrow to the string; then remember, and have to lay the bow down."

Bitz, habitually, changed my life. She would be sleeping peacefully beside me on the couch; I'd be afraid to get up and return to my desk, knowing that, if I moved, she would follow. Thought after feeling after action — the daily rescue from the roof, the endless openings of cans of tuna, her waiting for me at the gate when I pulled into the driveway — had my scatterbrained cat for their object. Now she is gone. For me to move on will mean resetting my sights on a target much bigger than my boundless love.

She wasn't just a cat. She is dead. But I still picture the look she gave me as her eyes flamed up one last time in our driveway. Her look — of love, of fury — seemed to say, "We had great joy of my body. Now, scatter the ashes."

DEAR DEAD PERSON

August 5, 2004

Sometimes when I start to write a letter I type, by accident, *Dead* instead of *Dear*. *Dead Grandfather*, I once wrote (when he was still alive). I couldn't think of anything to write after that, just stared at those black words on the white page remembering what he told me the day I caught my first perch off the dock in Fulford Harbour on Salt Spring: *the taking of a life is not such a difficult thing.*

"Dear is how you begin letters, even if you don't know the person, even if you don't like them, and Dear is what they call you when they write back," Kathy Page says, in her novel *Alphabet*. I remember making my daughter write a letter to the owners of a health food store she had B&E'd and also one to the police officer who didn't press charges. She refused to write "Dear Constable X . . . " because, she said, she didn't think of him as dear.

"Nobody writes letters anymore." How many times a day do I hear people say that? A few of my oldest friends here on Haida Gwaii still don't have electricity. For them, at least, technology has not killed off the ancient and noble art of letter-writing.

This morning as I sat in my chair, the sun filling to bursting my beautiful house, I found a Chinese proverb: *You cannot stop the birds of sadness from flying over your head, but you can stop them from nesting in your hair.* I went for a walk: the little patches of foam were moving up and down the beach, like soft icebergs, as the waves lolled in over the sand. I counted 125 young eagles at the Sangan River mouth, then gave up counting.

I have been writing for three hours in the mornings and then going for walks (by the cannery, and by the seaplane base in Masset Harbour) looking for eagle down. I watch ravens cavort in pairs above my head while I pick the down from the grasses. When I told my mother — she arrived two days ago and is staying at a B&B up the road — that one day I would have enough to make myself an eagle down pillow, she said, "Won't you have to sterilize it?"

Last night we went to Moon Over Naikoon for dinner, and shared a table with an ex-Vancouver city cop and his wife who were having an anniversary, and a Buddhist army officer who works for the Department of National Defense. I asked the cop's wife how they had come to move up here — she said they wanted to get away from their kids. Their "big night" when they were first married (she reminisced) was to buy a Duncan Hines Chocolate Chip Cookie Mix, bake the cookies until they weren't quite done, and eat them whilst they watched a video. Sweet, in an uncomplicated way. I made the mistake of saying I felt more sympathy for Osama bin Laden that I did for George Bush.

Most of the wild Island women I know are smitten with Osama bin Laden. Who can blame them, that famous clip on TV where he gallops across the desert on a flat-out Arabian stallion, robes billowing in the hot wind under a blue, unappeasable sky. Compare that to Bush in spurs and a cowboy hat in a western saddle with sweaty chaps.

The face of Osama bin Laden bears a striking similarity to our conceptions of Jesus. He has playful eyes — slightly feminine even — a beard that bespeaks a thoughtful piety. A smile half-dressed as a look of concern with a warning tossed in. Confronted by the bewildering benevolence of this face, even as he makes threats on all our lives, I can easily imagine him as a lover of many women, carefully brutal at some moments and solicitous at others.

August 6, 2004

This morning the phone rang early, waking me from a dream: I was racing, in a car, to get "somewhere". Here, where I am, where else? Cops kept pulling me over, taking my license plate number, issuing me tickets, so I abandoned the car and started crawling instead, on my hands and knees. I was getting so tired . . . a Buddhist monk approached me and said, "Stand up, you don't need to crawl. I will walk with you." He led me up some stairs to the front door of a monastery, which was like the gateway to another world. He said, "Here is our daily news. Our news of the world." I looked up and saw wind chimes!

Every day for the past week I've been driving to Masset to try and find a newspaper for my mother. Yesterday (Thursday) they finally got Monday's paper and then Mum said she didn't want old news even though I said the news never changes. It's just more bad news, anyway. Who needs the *Sun* when you have the wind?

My early morning phone call: an editor from *Saturday Night* magazine, wanting to know how I would dress for a "hot Saturday night date". Say what? A toque, pair of jeans, lumberjack shirt missing three of its five buttons, and gum-rubber boots.

Where would I be going — her next question — on my hot Saturday night date? I told her if I got lucky I'd be out picking eagle down off the wild pineapple grass, looking for tail feathers up Kliki Damen.

We talked for an hour; the editor, at the end of the conversation, felt renewed (she said), and I felt drained. I wanted to say to her, "Next time, write me a letter, please."

I've been thinking about the difference between letters and phone calls. Letters are reflective, phone calls reactive. Email is probably more direct than anything written by other means, but also reactive, and likely to inspire a similar response. It allows for spontaneity and the immediacy of speech but (alas) little time for reflection.

A letter is such a real, concrete thing. It doesn't vanish like conversation. We tend to keep letters even if we shouldn't (they can get us into trouble, if we're honest, and another person reading that letter can easily take something innocent "the wrong way"). When you tuck a letter away and find it, years later, it may not be what you remember being said, but there it is — evidence! You won't easily forget the people who have written to you, either.

Philip Larkin writes about "a world in which letters were greedily received and faithfully dispatched; in which the telephone was an expensive and barbarous mode of communication . . . and letters were relied on to combat the ills of daily existence." I have to ask myself, what is it in us that allowed the telephone, and email for that matter, such an easy takeover? I admit I put off writing letters — most letters — for as long as I can. And I don't know why I think of letter-writing as an onerous task, when, if I force myself to sit down to write, I fall into a trance of pleasure that is — restorative. Why do I fight myself? Why the divided will?

Oh the endless litany of *whys* that echo through the emptiness!

I have been missing Bitz. The hemlock she used to climb (and get stuck in) is outside my bedroom window. I can still see part of the ladder I built trying to climb up the tree to get her down.

I read this in *Buddha's Nature: Evolution as a Practical Guide to Enlightenment*, and it is helping me cope:

Regard your personality as a pet. It follows you around, anyway, so give it a name and make friends with it. Keep it on a leash when you need to and let it run free when you feel it is appropriate. Train it as well as you can but always remember your pet is not you. Your pet has its own life and just happens to be in an intimate relationship with you.

Who are you? It's YOUR PERSONALITY that has the terrible angst, not you!

So I have started practising having Bitz as my personality, beside me on a leash, getting under my feet. I have to laugh at myself. Why did I want to climb trees and not come down? Why did I want to run onto the road and die? Why did I want to cause ME such terrible grief?

Still, I look up into the sky and miss my personality, my dear, dead, scatterbrained friend.

What I want most is to spring out of this personality
then to sit apart from that leaping.
I've lived too long where I can be reached.

— Rumi, "Unseen Rain"

August 8, 2004

I went to visit my friend Helen yesterday. She told me about listening to the Nobel Prize ceremony on Radio Sweden (the fact that she owns a battery-powered transistor radio qualifies her as one of the few technological, pioneering friends I refer to in the first section of this book) in the middle of the night. J.M. Coetzee won, but nobody knew if he'd turn up to receive his prize, since he is known as being a recluse. He did show, and he gave a speech. He said, "We do it for our mothers. We do it for our mothers. Mummy, mummy, I won a prize." Then he put on a different voice. "That's nice, dear. Now shut up and eat your carrots before they get cold!"

Helen also talked about her sister's eccentric son, Duncan, who is in his early twenties and is "too brilliant to tie up his shoe laces" and lives in New Zealand where a big fuss is being made about Genetically Altered Foods. A woman was on the radio saying that if people ate Genetically Modified Foods you'd have women with three breasts, and so on.

There was an anti-GMO rally and Duncan went to it with a banner that read, "I'm for GMO Foods. Bring on the three-breasted women", and was attacked by a giant carrot. He had to be hauled away by the police — for his own protection.

Today the sun is brilliantly out so I am disorderedly affected. I suppose I will have to go for a walk: when it rains I can stay quiet and inside — my house and my self.

Meanwhile (technology beckons), I must check my email.

August 9, 2004

I should never check my email. Someone sent me a link to a site called Death Clock.com where you fill in your birthdate, age, weight, whether you are a smoker or non-smoker and then your "mode" (I wonder if they meant "mood"?) — a choice between: NORMAL, OPTIMISTIC, PESSIMISTIC, SADISTIC — click on "Reality Check" and are told the date of your pending demise. Since they didn't offer MASOCHISTIC I chose PESSIMISTIC (being a realist) and (how is this for a reality check?) I am going to die on March 5th, 2010.

Not enough time. I cheated death and changed my mode midstream, chose NORMAL, and got a new lease on life: May 24th, 2030. I decided I will be NORMAL from now on. A small compromise, if it buys me time. Plus, I intend to cheat . . .

But, I couldn't resist, I went back online later and changed my "mode" to OPTIMISTIC. Having committed to a bright and cheery outlook, I shall live almost another fifty years — 'til August 9th, 2043.

Finally I chose SADISTIC as a mode (even though I'm not). I am going to die on May 24th, 1990. And just as I was sitting there thinking, "I've been dead for fifteen years, that explains my mode!" another message popped up on the screen: "I'm sorry but your time has expired. Have a nice day!"

August 12, 2004

The muffler fell off my truck on the dark road Friday night. We'd been out to Yakan Point to watch the meteor deathfest. When I didn't see a falling star, I started wondering why I needed to see a star fall. Why wasn't I satisfied with stars just being up there? Again, it's the discrepancy between the way things are, and the way we want them to be, that causes such suffering.

Home from doing errands in Masset. Sophie wanted to eat, so I had to go to the bank — the kind that lends money, not the kind that holds up the river. (My neighbour distributed a pamphlet called HOW TO HOLD UP YOUR BANK. Many of us along the Sangan are losing land because of global warming, which is causing higher tides and, of course, erosion.) Money flowing from my wallet the way the water eats up the Sangan-bank on the incoming tide.

I don't worry about money when I'm here. I just spend it, not thinking about where more will come from. I am rich — in eagle feathers and moon shells, agates, and all-alone stones. I have these spread out on my table and, in the midst of them, a crumpled five dollar bill I pulled from a sandy pocket, and some change. Which is more real? More valuable? If I tried paying my ICBC bill with eagle feathers I guess I wouldn't have license plates. On the other hand, if eagle feathers were valid currency anywhere in this world, it would most likely be here in Masset.

I went grocery shopping for meat, because I am having neighbours for dinner who still think a vegetarian is someone who can't shoot a deer. Masset must be the only place in the world, too, where, in 2004 you say, "Are these the right kind of pork chops to cook with that can of mushroom soup recipe?" and the butcher puts together his thumb and index finger and kisses the air, and says, "Yessssss! Exactly right for the mushroom soup recipe!"

August 15, 2004

"I've found everything washed up on the beach here except a body," my friend, Jim, told me when he stopped by for coffee yesterday morning: he spent a couple of winters caretaking a fishing lodge off the west coast. Last winter he found dozens of left footed Nikes, after a container ship from Japan went down. Also a First Aid kit that contained 10,000 hits of codeine, "enough for us to party for a week." His girlfriend,

Barb, rescued a whole case of Pond's Face Cream and sent a jar to each of her friends for Christmas.

August 17, 2004

Outside I saw a pileated woodpecker pecking at the tree Bitz always climbed, and I thought — how can I stop the birds of sadness from pecking at my brain?

Every five seconds some large flying insect hurls itself into one of my windows, a bang here and a crash there. Maybe they are the souls of old spirits of the land, trying to find a way in. Maybe it is my own soul, trying to find a way out.

Sophie just waded back across the river in a velvet teddy, a pair of baggy shorts, and gumboots. Haida Gwaii *haute couture*. She has been trying to make friends with the tourist boys on the opposite bank who drive all-terrain vehicles and roar up and down the river making a terrible noise and destroying the environment — the sea asparagus and the tender beach-carrot plants. After that they shoot their paintball guns at the stars.

August 25, 2004

Big storm last night so I went beachcombing this morning. Amongst the plastic shopping bags and Javex bottles, fishing floats, and frayed pieces of dock rope, I found other, important, treasures — a can of Turtle Wax, a baby's car seat, a package of midnight-blue condoms, a half bottle of Bacardi, and a broken piece of plywood with the words FORBIDDEN ZONE. This is my news from the outside world, my daily mail, posted anonymously and arriving by accident, connecting me to the lives of strangers on far away shores.

The ocean giveth but it also taketh away. I almost lost my pick-up driving home along the beach after I misjudged the tide.

Jim stopped by to say that after years of looking he had finally found a body — an eighteen-year-old kid who had been missing since June, when he had driven off the end of the pier after celebrating alcoholically the night of his graduation.

Jim showed me the boy's waterproof watch. Still ticking. He'd strapped it to his wrist.

Dear Dead Person: Soon there will be a shrine at the end of the dock where you failed to negotiate your turn. A white cross festooned with yellow ribbons, and the only photograph of you where you are not under the influence, the one where you already look embalmed, in your graduation gown. There will be scraps of poetry from girls scotch-taped to the cross, and awkward messages from your drinking buddies, HAVE A GOOD ONE, SEE YA AROUND DUDE. There will be bunches of cut flowers in tipping mason jars, a pot of chrysanthemums that will soon die because no one will walk that far to water them, and bouquets of artificial flower-sorrow in faded pinks and blues. The quality of the grief will have a kind of Value Village aura, which will make it — to the passing stranger — all the more sad.

The sun is out today, the calm after last night's storm. I lay awake most of the night, listening to the wind, the sound of the rain on the roof better than a thousand mothers.

Printed and bound
in Boucherville, Quebec, Canada by
Marc Veilleux Imprimeur Inc.
in August, 2005